GARDEN RAIL
IN FOCUS

Tag Gorton

ATLANTIC PUBLISHERS

Front Cover -

A late summer afternoon on the Foxfields Light Railway sees Dave Wilding's newly rebuilt Roundhouse 'William', inch onto the trestle bridge outside Soller station, prior to backing onto the last passenger working of the day. Note the exquisite scratch-built valve gear and motion that has now been fitted.
John Fox

Back Cover -

Top: Lady Anne waits for the whistle to depart from Seven Beach with her short mixed train, whilst Hunslet *Cackler* blows off steam while awaiting the road for the shed. Many people move into 16mm scale railways to capture the ethos of real steam running - and this photograph certainly captures the spirit of garden scale steam!

Lower: The 'Indian' engine, number 724 *Gwalior* was acquired from that country and is a recent addition to the stable of the Southern Cross Railway. Blasting uphill over the last remaining large trestle at Powderwash she has sixteen complaining oil tanks in tow.

Atlantic Publishers

83 Parkanaur Avenue, Southend-on-Sea, Essex SS1 3JA

ISBN: 1 902827 12 0

© Atlantic Editions Limited 2005

British Cataloguing in Publication Data

A catalogue for this book is available from the British Library

Printed by The Amadeus Press Ltd, Bradford

Contents

Introduction

Curving away into the shadowy quiet of a deep cutting, the moss covered narrow gauge rails in front of us are, rather obviously, not host to a busy commuter service. The 'Beware of Trains' sign by the kissing-gate is almost superfluous, as any activity on this quirky little railway is hardly likely to be quick enough to catch a resident taking the short cut to 'The Sailors Rest' at Longlands, or the odd rambler looking for the path to the crumbling remains of Wheal Ale engine house. There is however, still a regular service of sorts. Steam powered passenger trains connect the villages and hamlets in the hinterland of this inaccessible corner of South East Cornwall with the junction at Saltash, still taking residents to work and sailors from the nearby Royal Dockyard to the 'recreational facilities' at Longlands. Mineral trains are run as required to service the quarry at Forder and, in the summer, the beginnings of a tourist trade have meant the strengthening of regular passenger services.

The line runs through a granite strewn, heavily wooded Cornish landscape, where a light sea breeze can set the trees rustling and the summer sun will dapple the lush greenery beneath them. The old linesman's hut at the mouth of the cutting gets rustier every year and the granite cottage beside the track looks an ideal place for an old sailor to spend a happy retirement. One can hear the short service trains whistle their way through the tunnel at Trehan and can follow their progress by means of the steam exhaust above the cutting before a train actually comes into sight, easing asthmatically round the tight curve under the Chapel Bridge before drawing up at Trematon station…

When I was a child, this sort of sight was common all over these islands. No more alas, but nowadays I can sit with a cup of tea and replicate those far off days in my small back garden, watching the trains go by. This reproduction of a Cornish steam-powered backwater is my own idea of a garden railway and it is built and run to suit me. Some may prefer the colourful and efficient metre gauge railways found in Continental Europe whilst others favour standard gauge trains in action on a double track main line. I make no value judgements here - the world of garden railways is a pastime and hobby that is both creative and imaginative rather than competitive.

A Whole New Dimension

Once upon a time railways in gardens were the only game in town - other than a small selection of live steam 'dribblers' designed to run on the playroom floor and simple toy representations of early steam locomotives for the offspring of the seriously rich. Within

Longlands is a popular destination for sailors on shore leave, keen to avail themselves of the recreational facilities provided by Madam Esmerelda Lash, proprietor of the 'The Sailors Rest'. Well-known 45mm gauge modeller John Rogers may often be seen here, sleeping off his pub lunch on a station bench.

Curving under Chapel Bridge with a rake of old four-wheelers forming the homeward bound school train from Saltash Junction, 0-4-0 *Les Grant* creeps asthmatically past the fixed distant as it approaches Longlands.

living memory however, the accent has most certainly, been on the indoor model railway. These were initially tinplate, usually Gauge O and designed to attract purchasers from what was broadly termed the middle classes, who were the only ones with the disposable income to spend on such fripperies for their children.

The rise of the post-war consumer society and improvements in manufacturing technology fuelled production of smaller scale models and the 00 gauge 'tabletop' railway was found to be more suited both to the constraints of modern housing and to the depth of the purchaser's pocket. Railways built in the garden however, tended still to be the preserve of the more affluent and perhaps more eccentric section of the modelling population and the flag, over these wilderness years, was largely kept flying by those who modelled in Gauge 1.

When I first moved into the garden some twenty odd years ago, I was attracted by the possibility of comparatively affordable live steam. The simple little meths fired pot boilers and the first of the gas fired locomotives then available were really only representations of the real thing, but a further attraction was that they were built on a narrow gauge format - which meant that a railway powered by live steam could be constructed in the smallest of gardens - and mine was pretty small! Many people were also moving into the garden using the G-scale products of Ernst Paul Lehmann Patentwerk (LGB) and its derivatives - which again were built to a narrow gauge format, but representing the metre gauge railways in Europe. These models were (and are) in fact very well detailed and, despite being electrically powered, were certainly more than rugged enough to run in the great outdoors and again, the narrow gauge outline meant that a railway constructed in this way would take up comparatively little space.

The Camera Lens is Pitiless

Those first railways of the 'new wave' like the models themselves, were comparatively simple, but the very fact that these railways ran in the open air and in natural light, provided a whole new dimension of realism. An early (in garden railway terms) copy of *Railway Modeller*, featured an article on Peter Dobson's 16mm scale garden railway and I remember it particularly, because the live steam locomotives and their trains were running through a station that had an awning, built very simply, using curly shelf brackets to represent the Victorian ironwork so often seen on this type of railway structure.

Now this was a very basic construction and, if built for a scenic indoor line, would certainly have turned up a few noses, but in the real lighting of the great outdoors, this model captured the atmosphere of a 'Corris Railway' type awning to perfection! Now I can and do admire the excellent work produced by our centrally heated fellow travellers, but while our eyes and imagination can deal with the artificial light when inspecting someone's indoor pride and joy - the camera lens is pitiless and photographs taken in artificial light look flat and lifeless.

The kissing-gate at Longlands takes the pedestrian across the coal yard and into Station Road. This is usually a short cut to 'The Sailors Rest' or takes one across the higher moor to the old engine house at Wheal Ale.

Some years ago I wrote a book called *Steam in Your Garden* - now out of print. This was originally made available from the Railway Book Club and, for many months, photographs from this minor work were lifted to illustrate the modelling section of the Club newsletters. Now I don't flatter myself that I am anything like a professional photographer, but you see my pictures of railways looked 'right' because the light was right. As garden railway modellers we have this huge advantage - our railways are real - they run through the real world and in real weather and are not preserved in the artificially lit aspic of a summer day in 1937 on a dusty baseboard in the back bedroom.

Running in the Open Air

Modern garden railways, of whatever scale or gauge, have moved on considerably in the last twenty years or so. Some of the first G-scale railways seen in magazines, consisted of little more than fixed track sections laid temporarily on a freshly mown lawn on a summer afternoon, with perhaps just a few Pola buildings to add verisimilitude. 16mm scale steam lines were rather different to this, largely I suppose, because there was no 'clip-together' track available but, with a few honourable and far-seeing exceptions, the idea of constructing a believable scale world with living scenery and 'all weather' buildings, had been taken up by very few people in any scale.

This was perhaps because the idea of running in the open air was novelty enough in those days - and for many people the added dimension of live steam was the main priority, with one's imagination providing all railway infrastructure other than required civil engineering. With the increasing sophistication of both electrical train control and commercial radio controlled steam locomotives, it became very much easier to run a railway in the garden and, increasingly, the refugees from the back bedroom

were applying their indoor modelling skills to their outdoor enterprises. The idea of modelling the complete railway scene in the garden has gradually taken hold - as it did in its turn for indoor railways between the wars. There are perhaps, other reasons. I, for instance, had a large collection of N Gauge stock but, even in this small scale, the demands of a growing family meant that I never really had the space to actually build a model railway - until I moved into the garden!

'Yer Average' Garden Railway

The size and presence of the larger outdoor scales has not only attracted modellers from the smaller scales but has drawn in people who have no modelling background at all, but who do have an interest in railways of all types. Those who construct a garden railway tend to be far removed from the (in any case inaccurate) perception of the railway modeller as a loner who locks himself away in the attic. Take a look at any of the hundreds of garden meetings held up and down this United Kingdom! A more sociable and disparate mix of men and women it would be difficult to find.

Perhaps because of this there can be no such thing as 'yer average' garden railway. The railways in this book are of varying scales and gauges. They range from the expansive wide-open spaces of the mountain road on the Southern Cross to the industrial narrow gauge and homely little steam engines of the Sylvan Heights Tramway. This is not a book about the construction of garden railways. My hope is that, like me, you will enjoy these photographic essays for their own sake and perhaps gain inspiration and not a few ideas for your own great railway adventure. Each railway herein is entirely individual to its builder and all are very different, but each and every one of them has that single ingredient essential to the creation of a satisfying garden railway - imagination!

The Southern Cross Railway

Nick Trudgian was brought up in a part of Plymouth that was, in those days, totally surrounded by railways. He attended Art College in Plymouth and Cornwall, and is nowadays a freelance artist somewhere 'up country', where he produces superbly atmospheric paintings of famous warplanes, in many cases signed by the original pilots and bomber crews. These works are sought after all over the world and an idle ten minutes on a web browser will find many examples of his paintings.

Nick is perhaps one of the 'new wave' of garden railway builders who like to model the whole railway and its environs, rather than 'just' the trains. A committed railway model-maker, he has, since discovering garden railways, created one of the most impressive examples I have ever seen. Peter Jones has called the garden railway a three dimensional art form and I think, after losing yourself in the following photographs, you will agree that this delightful mix of art and engineering - is just that!

I have built model railways all my life and became interested in garden railways in 1994 after seeing the one at Hampton Loade on the Severn Valley Railway. The original part of my line was built on the remains of an air raid shelter that had been part of what was once a Battle of Britain airfield. The line kept growing, eventually swallowing up the vegetable garden and

Enyati yard is where trains are prepared for their journey to the coast and there is usually plenty of activity. Today is no exception. On track 2 an empty hopper train has just arrived being banked in the rear by two of the 4-6-0's coupled back to back. Their next duty will be to take out the oil train being marshalled by the 2-6-0 Number 13 on track 4. Another 4-6-0 is busy further down the yard.

SOUTHERN CROSS RAILWAY
STORMBERG REEF GOLD MINES

LIVE STEAM OR BATTERY POWER.
LENGTH OF MAIN LINE .... 960 ft. [292m].
DESIGN .... END TO END.
ONE COMPLETE CIRCUIT .... 1700 ft. [518 m].
TRACK .... PECO G45.
GAUGE .... 45mm.
SCALE .... 1:24 AND 1:20.
MINIMUM RADIUS MAIN LINE .... 10 ft. [3m].

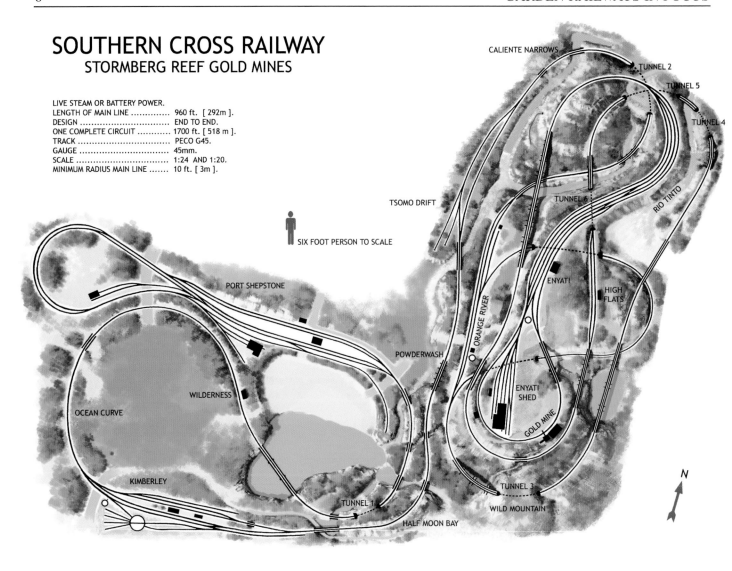

SIX FOOT PERSON TO SCALE

part of the lawn. I built it all myself. Being self-employed, I like to spend each morning in the garden building the railway, then spend the rest of the day trying to catch up on my real work.

The track-bed is made from concrete lintels on concrete block piers on concrete foundations. The main line is just under 1000ft long, an 'end to end' design, Peco track, 45mm gauge. An out and back return trip over the line is 1700ft and takes about 20 minutes at a realistic speed. No track power, it is either live steam or battery power. Minimum radius on the mainline is 10ft.

I am lucky to have a small group of friends who visit regularly to run trains and they bring a lot of their own stock with them. We try to run the railway in a realistic manner and, being a single line with crossing loops, we have to work as a team. Waiting in a loop for a train to pass is a part of the fun. We like to run big trains, often more than twenty wagons long, the record being seventy-eight, measuring 115ft in length.

The Old Ways Prevailed

I have only the most ghostly memories of the last days of real working steam in the south west of England. I was born just a little too late. Preserved railways and picture books of what

once had been were some compensation and they nurtured my passion for steam but throughout my teen years I had a growing frustration that I had missed out on something very special. One memorable afternoon my father returned from the library with a book about foreign steam trains. Not my cup of tea I thought but I showed polite interest and was surprised to find these alien locos rather appealing. It was also a revelation to find that many of them were still running, not yet consigned to history. Well it took a few more frustrating years to scrape the money together but as soon as I was able I began to travel overseas to a few of those places where diesels hadn't made their unwelcome appearance and where the old ways prevailed. Here steam trains were still working as they always had, just a part of the landscape, generally unloved and unnoticed by a local population to whom they were at best merely a form of transport and at worst a filthy inconvenience. This was the honest reality of steam and I savoured every bit of it especially knowing full well that the writing was on the wall even in these far outposts. For me it was like a ride back in time and although none of my experiences could exactly re-enact what I had missed in Britain I was seeing at first hand what steam powered railways were all about.

Top: One of the shed master's favourites, oil fired Baldwin 4-6-0 number 17, is seen heading towards her first stop at Wilderness with the late morning departure from Port Shepstone. At this point the line is just a few feet above the tidal river and from here a relentless climb takes the train into an ever more remote world. The lush sub-tropical foliage of the coast gives way to pine forest and tumbling rivers and beyond that a landscape of snow capped mountains, high meadows and hanging mists.

Lower: Shay number 15 *Zuma*, is an illusive engine spending most of her life in the sun-dappled shade of forest sidings. She is a logging engine, only venturing onto the main line when sufficient log cars have been loaded to warrant a trip to the millpond. Standing in for a broken down loco, *Zuma* makes a rare appearance at the head of a work train photographed here leaving the west end of Tunnel 2.

Right: Built in 1876 the 2-6-0 number 13 is a remarkable survivor. Once very much the 'Wild West' engine the years have taken their toll. She has lost her massive diamond stack, cow catcher and fancy domes but she still has an undeniable elegance and can give the other engines a run for their money.

Above: Not for the faint hearted the transition from Tunnel 3 to the giddy heights of Wild Mountain trestle is a sudden one. Nothing has fallen off here - yet, but the drivers still take it steady particularly with the shed master's pride and joy, loco number 18. Woe-betide anyone who even scratches the paintwork.

Left: The powerful Mallet tank number 19 is at the Number 4 Shaft loading point at Enyati carefully spotting hoppers under the chutes. This is the highest point on the entire railway so gravity not only assists in loading but also in getting the precious cargo to the coast.

Right: **Kicking up the dust and sending the gophers scurrying number 18 comes clattering down through Rio Tinto with eighteen empty hoppers. As quickly as she appeared she has gone again leaving only singing rails and a haze of perfumed smoke. Tranquillity returns to this remote valley but how long is it until the next train? They mostly run as required on this line so it's anyone's guess.**

Lower: **Their exhaust is like gunfire ricocheting from the cliffs in this deepest part of the canyon as Baldwins 18 and 1320 struggle to keep their oil train moving. From the warmth of the evening sun the engines are about to enter the cold blackness of Tunnel Number 2 and to stall in there would be most unpleasant. Thankfully today the wagons keep rolling, but only just, and the sun has dipped behind the mountains by the time the brakevan passes by.**

Railways in their Rawest Form

Of the lines I saw the ones that I grew to like most were the self-contained industrial railways. Away from the glamour of the main line or the charm of the rural branch lines these operations somehow captured the very essence of railways in their rawest form. Perhaps they were built to carry gold or lumber, coal or sugar cane but what they invariably had in common was that they were entire railway systems built on a local scale. There would be engine sheds, workshops, a source of traffic and a destination. Trains would often be hauled by oddball collections of hand-me-down engines painted in whatever colours the owners (or sometimes the driver) fancied. When it came to building a model railway these lines gave me all the inspiration I needed, with the added bonus that nobody could ever fault me on research because on such railways anything goes. For my line's main industry I chose gold mining and set it in a mountain location so that I could have bridges and tunnels, forest and canyons. If asked where the line is supposed to be I say the Southern Hemisphere, hence the name, but won't be pressed any further. I don't want to be restricted by modelling anything particular, but try to capture that essence of a steam railway.

Incense of Coal Smoke

Ultimately this is my railway. I can sit on a rock, coffee in hand, and admire a work worn engine toiling through its miniature domain with that uncanny degree of realism, which only the natural light and living landscape of a garden railway can provide.

Above: **Stormberg Reef's most powerful loco is this 2-6-6-2 Mallet now running with a South African Railways tender and making twenty-eight wheels in total. Capable of handling forty hoppers Number 226 comes into her own when traffic levels are high but otherwise she is found out of use in Enyati shed as her coal consumption is huge. Seen here at the line's lowest point on Wilderness River Bridge, the hills will soon echo with the distinctive rhythm of her double exhaust.**

Left: **Being the halfway point along the line, Orange River is a busy crossing place. Here a long train of empties, banked in the rear by Number 19, waits patiently for the afternoon oil train to pass headed by the big Mallet No.226. Up trains take water and have their fires cleaned in readiness for the stiffest climb ahead and down trains get a chance to cool their brake blocks.**

Right: Two heavy tank engines, numbers 14 and 19, join forces to lift this lengthy train of empties through Tsomo Drift. Their labouring exhausts fill the scene with coal smoke and a noise loud enough to shake loose rocks from the cliffs. The sound is suddenly muffled as each engine plunges into Tunnel Number 2 but the smoke lingers long after the last wagons have passed by and the old canyon returns to its slumber.

Lower: Towards the end of the day at Port Shepstone Shed and the yard is full of engines ready to return to the mine. Trains of empties will soon work back in quick succession but it will be well after sunset before the sound of the last of them fades into the night.

Left: **In the depths of winter the line presents a very different picture. The cheery paintwork of number 18 helps to enliven this bleak landscape at Powderwash on a bitter morning. Summer might be more pleasant for photographers but for the railway the wheels have to keep turning whatever the weather.**

Lower: **Rolling into town at Port Shepstone comes the red painted number 17 with an oil train bound for the jetties. Three empty ore trains are being prepared for their return journeys and with a surplus of locos to hand the yard pilot takes a rest over at the shed. This harbour-side town owes its existence to the mines and railway, there was little here before gold was discovered in the Stormberg Range and prospectors hurried in to seek their fortune.**

Right: **From Tsomo Drift the line follows a horseshoe curve towards Orange River replacing the zigzag that used to link them and which caused endless delays. At busy times however this can still be a bottleneck. Baldwin 2-8-0's numbers 18 and 1320 are held at Tsomo because the hopper train ahead of them is taking water at Orange River and another down train is due. It's going to be a struggle to get those tank cars moving again on the stiff grade out of here.**

Mid-day at Port Shepstone shed finds number 18 *Cotopaxi* having a doze while her crew enjoy lunch at a nearby bar. This was once the only shed on the line but it proved hopelessly inadequate and now with the new and spacious shed at Enyati only the yard pilot and locos on the early up trains spend the night here.

My imagination allows me to complete the illusion. I can hear the whistles echo around the hills, picture the steam billowing into a cobalt sky - and delight in the incense of coal smoke. And so I am connected to my memories and lost in a pretend world where steam will go on forever.

Here are some pictures of the railway. The captions are written from the perspective of someone who is living in this make-believe land and are mostly born of my caffeine, or is it butane, induced state.

Above: The 'Indian' engine, number 724 *Gwalior* was acquired from that country and is a recent addition to the stable. Blasting uphill over the last remaining large trestle at Powderwash she has sixteen complaining oil tanks in tow.

Left: In high summer the Rio Tinto is little more than a stream so it is possible to stand beneath the girder bridge that connects Tunnels 4 and 5. The sun is also high enough at this time of year to illuminate the trains, albeit for the fleeting moments they take to leave one tunnel and plunge into the next.

The North Somerset Light Railway

Something I have noticed over the years, is that while there are many husband and wife 'garden railway builder' teams in the USA, they seem to be a comparatively rare phenomenon in the United Kingdom. In fact as *Alan Habgood* says, "It is relatively unknown in our circles to be married to a real railway partner. Janet is probably best known for organising the 2004 and 2005 16mm Association Conventions, but beyond that her involvement and knowledge of our hobby is stunning. She does not laugh from the shelter of the conservatory whilst I get soaked..."

After a nostalgic foray into collecting 00-gauge trains, Alan and Janet first moved into the great outdoors using Lima 0-gauge equipment, which resulted in a ground level garden layout that turned out to be not totally flat. Unfortunately, it was found that the tiny motors couldn't cope with the gradients and also, the low-lying track frequently flooded - a recipe for disaster!

Live steam garden railways were eventually discovered at the Donnington Model Engineering Show in 1996 where there happened to be a 16mm demonstration layout. They had actually been considering 5ins gauge, but upon finding that 16mm scale live steam locomotives were perfectly controllable, they both felt that a steam worked line in their garden at home would be feasible - and so it proved!

In fact *Alan and Janet Habgood's* garden is quite a difficult site for a garden railway, being almost totally enclosed and largely flat. This has meant that the railway has had to be constructed at waist level and, while it is perfectly possible to build a well-engineered line in this way, it is a rather more difficult job to make this type of construction both scenic and attractive.

I have chosen this railway to represent this form of construction because, as I think you will agree, they have succeeded brilliantly and I think this may be something to do with teamwork! While planning and construction was a joint effort, Alan tends to deal with the logistics while Janet's sharply observant eye has brought to life the various buildings, structures and scenes that she has built around the railway.

This railway, with the added attraction of lots of railway memorabilia, including cast iron signs, lamps and a fully restored Western Region semaphore signal - all set in a well tended garden - is a delight to visit and a pleasure to run on...

T he NSLR has long since been disconnected from its link with a bay platform at the nearby standard gauge Worle station. What remains is essentially a circular narrow gauge route encompassing some ⅓ mile with a further ⅕ mile taken up by loops and sidings. The 2ft gauge track was specially constructed into preformed sections by an engineering plant in Beer, Devon and shipped by barge up the Severn Estuary to Weston-super-Mare (suitable ballast was imported from a limestone quarry in Wells). Its success now lies in the linking of two busy little communities both situated just east of the more widely known Weston-super-Mare mainline station.

In its heyday the structures, sometimes of dubious architectural origin, were added as and when the railway's development dictated. Anything paintable tended to end up as near to a corporate livery as you could imagine - namely green, cream or both. This policy - if you can call an accident of evolution a policy - has resulted in the assembly of a wide and varying collection of buildings.

Motive power in the main comprises Welsh style 0-4-0s from all over the UK but mostly constructed in Doncaster with others having adopted sea legs for their journey from the Far East. All had to be chosen using a well considered formula of cost versus reliability. Liveries and lining schemes if in good condition tend to stay as upon arrival, however if they don't please the eye and surplus paint falls into skilled hands anything

could emerge, and it does! Similarly the coaching stock has no standard livery with paint schemes designed to cut a colourful but sometimes eye jarring swathe through the countryside. A return to normality is prompted by the goods section, which for years has been dipping into a massive stockpile of ex military battleship grey.

Above: Lady Anne waits for the whistle to depart from Seven Beach with her short mixed train, whilst Hunslet *Cackler* blows off steam while awaiting the road for the shed. Many people move into 16mm scale railways to capture the ethos of real steam running - and this photograph certainly captures the spirit of garden scale steam!

Left: Boxwall Junction seems busy this evening with locos down in the yard, Fletcher Jennings *Dolgoch* in the loop and Peckett No 1030 *Gamecock* departing with some of the NSLR's more draughty carriages - loads of narrow gauge atmosphere at this location.

Right: If you want to know the time ask a train driver! The 'strong arm of the law' witnesses *Lady Anne* at Seven Beach crossing as she eases her short train away from the station. Careful perusal will confirm that the signal box is fully fitted internally.

Lower: Summer colour on the NSLR - where garden and railway co-exist.

Ash Encrusted Shed Lines

This railway also enjoys a woman's creative touch as the signal box, cabin and both water towers were designed and built by the wife of the main railway director, with the sumptuous interior décor speaking volumes about her dedication to the railway.

It would be easy to assume that since its excommunication from the mainline, morale and standards would have deteriorated. On the contrary, the trackside spirit couldn't be stronger and has actually strengthened - but don't take my word for it - why not travel the railway under your own steam and see what you make of it?

All good journeys must start somewhere, so why not at a point considered by many to be of most interest - the engine shed. Of the three ash encrusted shed lines, only one is protected by a well equipped single road engine workshop situated somewhat precariously close to a sheer rock face. Having settled down since its long past quarrying career the structure seems moderately sound, save for the dislodging of some relatively small rock pieces by the ever expanding roots of the now resident vegetation. Never fear signs, warning of the dangers are strategically placed, thus ensuring that if you stand by one to read it you're definitely a gambler.

The engine shed was built using local stone to a Cornish design and topped with slate. The resultant building proves to be both charming and functional. Consider yourself honoured if you are invited onto the footplate of the next loco departing. The regulator is barely open as we chuff gently on towards the station. In all five sets of points will be encountered before you join the mainline the first task being to carefully navigate the

limited clearance past the goods shed. It also sits in the shadow of the cliff face and has an identical pedigree to the workshop. It's now busy with fruit, vegetables and fish from the locally run farm. Frantic as it may be there is always time to gather in the goods office around the ever-inviting coal fire.

Having arrived at Seven Beach station you will first encounter the stationmaster who genuinely looks as though he has been here since day one. It is a certainty that he will first ask, "Who gave you permission to ride the footplate?" and, even though you are a special guest, he will insist that you purchase a ticket.

A Wash of Soft Gas Light

Despite the officious nature of your first encounter (he's OK when you get to know him) Seven Beach is a typically homely and very narrow gauge station which was originally built in Norfolk but each piece was painstakingly numbered, moved and reconstructed to facilitate its second lease of life here at Seven Beach. Through a sense of sheer local pride, the interior is luxuriously furnished and is at its most attractive when bathed in a wash of soft gas light. Rather unusually it has three platforms, with the offside track passing between the outer two, plenty of length here for passengers to disembark. The station platform clock was badly jolted during the move causing the hands to jam so now all trains arrive and leave at 8:15.

It's 8:15 now, so it's time to sound the departure whistle leave the station and head past the Seven Beach signal box, this traditional timber constructed type box in common with the signal cabin at Boxwall Junction was designed by the wife of the main railway director and sits beside a busy level crossing. Its situation

Above: A summer evening on the platform at Seven Beach and there is plenty of activity for the waiting passengers to enjoy. Fletcher Jennings *Dolgoch* with too much pressure just to stand around, rolls effortlessly away with the 8:15. On the loop line No 3 *Lady Anne* has finished its roster and will return to the engine shed to make ready for another busy day tomorrow.

Right: Peckett No 1030 *Gamecock* clears the shed roads of slate wagons at the end of the day, the chuffing of this little locomotive sounding loud in the still of this summer evening...

Above: **Prior to the working day, three of the lines prettier locomotives wait for their call to duty. An oily rag (and lots of work) keeps them in pristine condition - in stark contrast to the area around the steam shed. The variations in colour and texture coupled with the carefully chosen detritus of the working shed contrast with the oily sheen of the well cared for locomotive paintwork.**

Left: **Hunslet *Elidir* is seen here awaiting servicing. They certainly knew how to make engines in 1889! This carefully observed cameo reflects a corner of a working shed.**

Right: **Hunslet No 493** *Elidir* **and Pecket No 1030** *Gamecock* **make a very lively start from Boxwall Junction with a mixed train. They are supposed to be working together but it sounds more like they are having a race.**

is idyllic as just across the line is a man-made pond, which, with its reed bed, swans, ducks and toads is a veritable wildlife sanctuary.

As the crossing gates close behind your train you will gather speed down a straight before turning east through quite a severe reverse curve - which is guaranteed to attack the wheel flanges and slow down any drivers who gathered momentum by storming up the straight.

The track then meanders through a densely wooded area and for a time disappears from view as it makes its way behind the local fish farm, which has, among others, a final holding tank containing some closely guarded and enormous specimens. There is no natural gradient on the site, so a flow of water has to be artificially created by the use of a coal fired steam pump. This is a very efficient beast, but none the less a good source of revenue for the local coal merchant.

Another tight pull to the left as we head north across the girder bridge, thanks to G Bear at Boxwalls Railway Salvage Yard. This structure was reclaimed from the mainline and sold to the NSLR. Consequently there is plenty of width, which easily accommodates the required loading gauge. The remaining space has been utilised in the provision of a bridge maintenance walkway erected along one side of the track. Despite 'staff only' signs this path is regularly used as an illegal route between the precariously narrow trackbed past the fish farm and the smallholding beyond.

Direct Contravention of Railway Regulations

And so to Boxwall Junction, a charming signal cabin and shelter sporting a surplus of green and cream paints, its location

nestled within varied woodland, making this junction halt a popular destination with locals and visitors alike. It has sufficient platform capacity to allow passing trains on a substantial loop, which remains from the long coal train days. At the bridge end of the platform is the lovingly tended stationmaster's cottage, a self-sufficient dwelling which has a well stocked vegetable garden and is situated adjacent to four walled enclosures, housing horses, cows, sheep, pigs and chickens. In direct contravention of railway regulations it is not unusual to find surplus produce

for sale on the platform and this popular activity continues without official comment.

This junction line originally passed through Boxwall Tunnel, being the only topographic deviation from the otherwise comparatively level landscape. This aptly named box sided tunnel was the single route through to share a platform with the mainline's Worle Station. Sadly five years ago the link proved to be uneconomic and the structure, whilst still a popular climb for hikers, has fallen into disrepair.

Left: **A view down the side of the engine workshop with the goods shed beyond The driver of the Fletcher Jennings** *Dolgoch*, **steps aboard to prepare the locomotive for the trip down to Seven Beach station to pick up a train.**

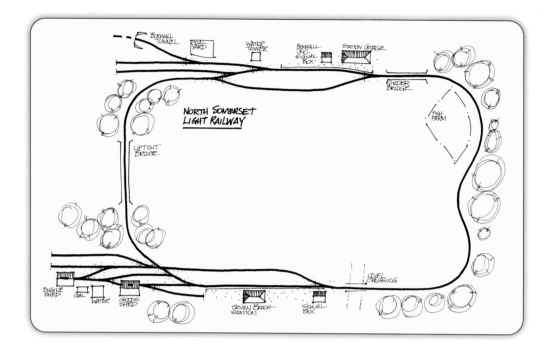

The tunnel now remains almost freestanding, as its original purpose was to cut a route through a mini slate mountain, which has been subsequently quarried out leaving the monolithic structure known as Boxwall Tunnel. Spoil from these workings can still be seen alongside the track on the west side, where some of it was used to fill a huge drainage ditch - thus preventing any further episodes of bovine aquatics. The old track that, rather inconveniently, crossed the yard of our friendly scrap merchant was removed even before the ink was dry on the closure notice.

Ghostly Dereliction

Be careful what you say though, because we are now passing the railway salvage yard belonging to Mr G Bear. What looks like *ad hoc* heaps of oddly shaped rusting metal, in practice translates into a very lucrative business so much so that he is now semi retired and can often be seen dozing in an armchair in front of his converted goods van/office. Despite this leisurely lifestyle he is a notorious light sleeper as his finely tuned hearing will very rapidly alert him to the money making potential of the very first ring of his telephone. A canny businessman, who specialises in buying surplus railway equipment from the NSLR, which is then stored in their own abandoned tunnel and miraculously sold back to them some time later.

Sharing the same corrugated access gate are the business premises of Mr A Bear, the brother of the scrap dealer, whose office is a disused lineside hut spruced up only by a brass 'office' plate bolted through - to prevent acquisition by his brother. Here stands a man who seems to have a teacup surgically fitted to his hand. He specialises in coal supplies and is the saviour of every open hearth in the vicinity. Having said that, since the link closure, all of the coal is brought to his yard by road and then loaded into open wagons held in either of the two goods sidings ready for movement to the engine shed on the west side.

It is also quite usual to see sack loads on board for dropping off at various locations around the line. This reciprocal arrangement grants the railway a very attractive coal price.

Having witnessed the ghostly dereliction of the tunnel, the line heads off through a sharp North Westerly bend before passing over a major engineering structure, a lift up hinged girder bridge which allows the passage of large traffic under and through the NSLR.

Seeing the shed roads to our right coming into view, means that our circular journey is drawing to a close. Stand firm in the cab as we shake, rattle and roll over the three sets of points, which will route us back into Seven Beach. The coaching stock will now be uncoupled whilst the loco runs round and backs on shed for refuelling. I hope you enjoyed the run and noticed that the stationmaster bade you a kind farewell, I told you he was OK if you got to know him!

Metre Gauge in the Côte d'Or

Bernard Déluard became a railway enthusiast at ten years of age, when his father started an O-gauge layout in the basement using Hornby & Jep equipment. Some years later Bernard had moved into HO scale and was building a second layout when marriage interfered with his modelling plans with a move to Dijon, in Burgundy, into a flat with no room whatever for a layout! Ten years later, his interest was reawakened when the children were offered a Playmobil train and Bernard started building a garden layout at his in-laws weekend house in the country.

Since that first foray into the garden with Playmobil, Bernard has gone on to produce one of the most atmospheric and evocative G-scale layouts I have ever seen. Redolent of pre-war French rural transport, this delightful line is captured on film by its creator, whose photographic skills most certainly match his eye for modelling. This is not so much a model railway, more a three-dimensional essay into days long gone.

As my home is now set in the Departement de la Côte d'Or, I naturally became interested in the history of the railways in this county, which were particularly developed between the years 1891 & 1953. Let me briefly point out a few significant historical landmarks. In the last two decades of the 19th century, France had decided to create a standard gauge railway network to link all the sous-préfectures. It was named the 'Freycinet Plan' after its founder, an engineer and Third Republic politician. But travelling across the countryside still remained difficult both for goods and passengers. This situation led many French *départements* to establish cheap narrow-gauge (almost always metre gauge) railway networks, often called 'tramways' because their tracks were set in the roadways. This network was particularly extensive in Côte d'Or, with up to 358 kilometres in 1922. Sadly, this was short lived, as most of it closed down when passenger services came to an end in 1933, leaving some freight services running on part of the network until WWII. During the German occupation, passenger service

was resumed with steam-hauled former luggage vans. In 1945, one railcar, which had been concealed during the war, was brought into service again until 1947. The ultimate operating line - namely the Dijon-Gevrey-Chambertin stretch, which had been built and electrified in 1909, closed down on May 5 1953.

I drew my inspiration from this network and have reproduced some of the buildings, many of which are still standing today. My G-scale rolling stock is being modelled after the locomotives and wagons operated locally. I started out with LGB rolling stock and have been adding equipment over the years, with a view to discarding all that is not French and concentrating on what was actually used in Côte d'Or.

The running shed currently employs two weathered and dirty-looking LGB 0-6-0 Corpet-Louvet tank locomotives complete with smoke unit and sound system, driver and fireman figures and with extra weight added to cope with steep gradients. There is another Corpet-Louvet locomotive, originally similar to the other two but which has been altered to make it look like

Left: **The grey No 20 Corpet-Louvet locomotive is hard put to work, holding back this long passenger train in the descent of the long downgrade to Noyers sur Couches station.**

Above: **Both trains are about to leave from Pruniers and passengers are hurrying to make sure that they don't miss the railcar to Soue at the end of the line.**

Right: **The platform and forecourt at Pruniers are now empty of passengers and the railcar and the goods train will soon leave in opposite directions... To take this picture, the photographer had to walk through the high grasses around the station.**

the real one, which is kept in working order in a museum devoted to metre gauge railways. I also have one weathered A80D Billiard railcar and its R210 trailer, both improved Apocopa kits, now complete with interior fittings.

American Kadee™ Coupling

As far as passenger trains are concerned, I have built from scratch two passenger carriages and one luggage van, faithfully reproducing those actually used in Côte d'Or from 1891 to 1933. Contrary to most passenger carriages on local metre gauge French railways at the time, these carriages had no platforms at each end but one central open-air platform, which was enclosed as early as the beginning of the 20th century.

An additional train is made of four carriages and one luggage van produced from Gecomodel kits. These were based on stock used in the Sarthe area. Home-made bogie passenger cars are in the making and will eventually provide a more realistic representation of the rolling stock actually used in Côte d'Or where both two-axle and bogie equipment coexisted.

Most freight trains are LGB products, which I have modified by reducing their wheelbase and installing a three-point bedplate. They have also been fitted with figures and freight, repainted and weathered. On all this equipment, I use the American Kadee™ coupling system as it is easy to operate and looks very effective - similar to a central buffer.

For this first decade of the railways history, electricity was supplied to the rails in the traditional manner and a remote control made it possible to operate the trains running in the area to which it was connected. This system has now been replaced by an LGB 'Multitrains System' meeting the DCC standards which provides the track with constant voltage necessary to permanently operate smoke units, sound generators and train lighting. Several train mouse controls can be plugged in outside the stations in sockets connected to the central station by armoured-cable.

Pruniers - Le Prelot

We will get on board the train in the former pigsty at the Soue station (Soue means pigsty in French), which consists of a few short lengths of track and a turntable to allow for shunting. It is also the place where all equipment and buildings are stored away when they are not in use and I use it as a workshop (for

Top Left: "Au revoir..." It is late afternoon and the train bound for Noyers sur Couches is leaving Pruniers station. The passengers will soon have to regain their seats when the train gets into a long tunnel.

Lower Left: A passenger train travelling through the Côte d'Or countryside, the exhaust echoing amongst the trees as it works up the steep incline to Soue station. To capture this service, the photographer has climbed up a tree alongside the track.

Right: Now down from his tree, the photographer has proceeded to the end of the masonry bridge to await the trains passing by the halt at Le Prelot; he arrived just in time to spot a short train from Noyers sur Couches about to stop briefly before entering the tunnel leading to Pruniers.

Lower: It was perhaps unfortunate that the elderly madame, caught enjoying the sun whilst dealing with a call of nature in this secluded place, should have her privacy invaded twice in the space of a few seconds! Perhaps she cannot hear the approaching train...

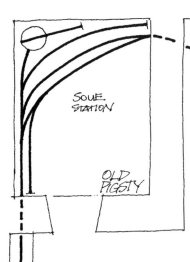
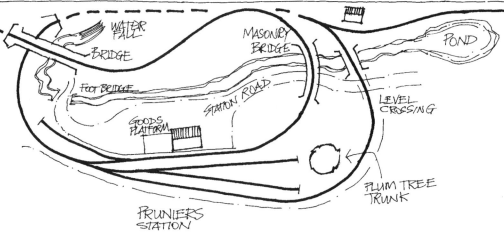
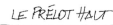

Above: **A long passenger train bound for Soue has almost reached Le Prelot after a steep incline. While passengers are getting on and off, the two employees will restore high pressure before entering the tunnel after the halt.**

Left: **Later our intrepid photographer was able to capture the departure of the train ex Noyers just before it disappeared into the tunnel on its way to Pruniers.**

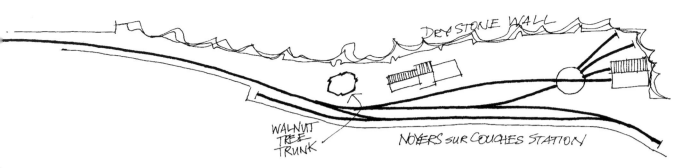

WALNUT TREE TRUNK

DRYSTONE WALL

NOYERS SUR COUCHES STATION

Above: **Some time later, a heavy lumber train is leaving Noyers sur Couches for Soue. An exceptional combination of two locomotives has been made necessary by the steep incline just out of the station.**

Right: **At Noyers sur Couches station, the fast railcar for Soue will leave first. The slow train will follow.**

minor repairs). It also houses the electrical supply point. Limited space and budget compelled me to use small radius LGB points in this area, but this station will soon be moved outside, to the end of a purpose-built future spur track.

Right after the station, a short tunnel cutting through the pigsty wall leads us onto a 1.20 metre-long metal bridge spanning both a stream fed by a waterfall and the Pruniers - Le Prelot track running along it. We then head down to Pruniers station via several 1 to 1.20 metre radius curves, crossing again on the way the stream and the road by means of a curving masonry bridge. The LGB metal bridge will give way to a homemade structure to be designed after a still extant one in Côte d'Or, now used as a road bridge. The masonry bridge is made of concrete first poured into plywood shuttering and then covered with a facing of engraved and painted PVC plates.

A stop at Pruniers, named after the plum tree that grows above it (Pruniers means plum tree in French) will enable us to witness the loading and unloading of timber, the main activity

Left: **It is raining at Noyers sur Couches station; to avoid passengers getting wet while boarding the train, the locomotive has pulled up the first carriage next to the station building.**

Lower: **At Noyers sur Couches station, workers are loading the luggage car, (a Gecomodel kit) which will be coupled at the head of the train. Such luggage cars used to be equipped with two dog kennels and a mail compartment - the one marked with the PTT inscription on the door.**

here. The building is an exact replica of the station in Pommard, the first station on the line linking Beaune to Semur-en-Auxois via Saulieu from 1891 onwards but better know for its world-class Burgundy wine! The outdoor plywood structure was adorned with plastic parts and artificially weathered to imitate the original building (as faithfully as possible).

With a blast from the whistle, the train leaves the station and will soon run under the metal bridge used at the beginning of the trip and into the longest tunnel on the line, a 3.78 metre-long curve with a 1.20 metre-radius at both ends. A short stop will then be made just outside the tunnel at the halt of Le Prelot - another faithful reproduction of a real way station serving a very small village near Champlitte, 60 kms north-east of Dijon.

Noyers-sur-Couches

From there, turning to the right would quickly bring us back to Pruniers Station, thus completing the loop on which my children used to operate their Playmobil train and where trains can still run in a circle.

But let's head down to the far end of the line along the garden wall, passing on the way a large bush acting as a transition between the two parts of the layout, until we finally reach the terminus station of Noyers-sur-Couches, (in French noyer = walnut tree) named after the big walnut tree under which it stands. We have come to the end of our 32.3 metre-long journey, dropping by 102 cms since we started.

This station consists of two buildings technically similar to that of Pruniers. The building housing the passenger services, the station master lodgings and the freight hall used to be commonplace on the local train network in Côte d'Or. Blueprints for such buildings dating back to the end of the 19th century have been stored in the archives of the coach company that took over from the railway company in 1949, enabling me to reproduce them accurately. The other building is a model of the depot at Champlitte (the terminus of the line originating in Dijon) in which, after the train service had closed down, coaches were parked until demolished in the 1980s.

Like in Soue Station, a turntable has been put in. This PVC structure slides round on top of a concrete pit. Such turntables are still in use on the Vivarais Railway in Ardèche in the South-East of France. The building of the layout started in 1988 with the short tunnel through the pigsty wall, followed by the longer one along the garden wall. The track bed, the road and the station yards are made of concrete poured over stone rubble. Carefully cemented stones were used for the riverbed, which was then painstakingly made waterproof by a coating of polyester resin. The over parts were filled in with earth and large stones to simulate rocks and hold up the earth.

Rail is 6mm High

The nature of the track varies depending on the stretch of line. The sleepers on the Soue - Le Prelot stretch as well as on the loop are LGB sleepers but the 8mm rail section was bought

Right: **At Noyers sur Couches station, the Corpet has been put ahead and two passengers are having a chat with the driver.**

Lower: **A country station! Passengers are in no hurry - they know the railway staff will wait.**

from a specialized dealer. The Soue & Pruniers points are also LGB products. All over rail is 6mm high and the sleepers are homemade, sawn from oak boards and then dipped for several weeks into a mixture of coal tar and 'Carbonyl' (a chemical used to deter insects from eating wood). The Noyers points are also home-made from 6mm-high rail. Ballast was obtained by sifting gravel through various riddles, which I had made myself by putting holes into flowerpot saucers. Cement water tied it together. Dirt, debris, plant matter and, above all, moss give it a very natural look and even require a complete cleaning of the track with a high-pressure hose every other year!

Platform edgings, lamppost and fence bases are made of painted PVC and are embedded into the ground. They are not removed and can even be stepped on! Rain, winter frost, sunshine and heat weather the structures in a natural process. Buildings and all other small elements such as fences, low walls, log-piles, lampposts, freight, goods and passengers are removed when not in use. Passengers and railway workers, often LGB or Preiser products, have been painted or repainted. Each one has been equipped with a 2mm wide brass peg under one foot which fits into 3mm-wide brass pipes embedded into the ground in various places so that they will not topple over!

Vegetation consists of bushes and perennials, carefully selected for their realistic aspect and either their slow growth or tolerance to pruning. Sickly-looking and dead plants must regularly be removed, pruning is essential in spring and must be carried on throughout the growing season, plant matter blown by the wind or carried by wild animals must be eliminated together with the massive amounts of nuts, plums and leaves in autumn which fall off the trees above the line. A big workshop vacuum-cleaner proves to be a very efficient ally in this endless fight repeated each time trains have not run for a few weeks or even a few days... The water in côte stream flows down into a

pond near the Le Prelot halt and, from there, is brought up to the top of the waterfall by a 12volt water pump designed for caravans. The pond acts as flush water basin, whose water level is regulated by a ballcock.

I have worked on this layout for seventeen years now from 1988 to 2005 and I have devoted many hours to this hobby, some of this time being spent at home in my flat and the rest during the holidays on the spot in the weekend house.

North Lindsay Light Railway

Nick Dew is married with two daughters, he keeps the wolf from the door by piloting a 44-tonne artic UK-wide on multi-drop deliveries a couple of days a week, whilst other time is divided between building and running the NLLR, writing occasional articles for *GardenRail* magazine, trying to maintain a run-down 17th century house in wildest North Lincolnshire, helping former colleagues with school musical presentations and undertaking the odd UK tour as an itinerant rock-drummer. He says that it certainly beats being on the treadmill and seems to work, in an interesting, but haphazard sort of way ...

Isn't it strange how perceptions of what you want change as the years roll by, perhaps reflecting the growth of family, for instance, or change of job; possibly a change of circumstances or moving house; maybe offspring entering further or higher education with all the financial ramifications that go hand in hand with that. When your progeny leave home, more or less permanently, and the mortgage is almost paid, it's time to review the last twenty-five years and wonder what happened to the grand plans you once harboured for an outdoor railway - you know, with chunky rolling stock and a real steam engine, or two. "Been there, done that, got the 'T'-shirt and the video", I hear you say. Meanwhile, the pioneers have forged ahead relentlessly, setting standards, drawing-in new members to the hobby, encouraging trade support, so that nowadays, you can consult a specialist dealer, write a cheque and have your dream railway delivered in boxes to use for a season or two before boredom sets in and you move quixotically on to the next 'in-thing'.

Those afflicted by such foibles, please move on and let those whose lives have been woven into the fabric of our great railway culture get on with building their dreams in the garden. We might never finish what we set out to do, but we'll have a whole lot of fun along the way and, at the end of the day, some sense of achievement.

There is a popular misconception that large amounts of money are needed to build and operate the garden railway of your dreams but it's the dreams that are really important, plus a little imagination - and that's all you need to get started. I remember sketching possible track layouts at a time when university had captured our eldest and was beckoning the second, consequently money was still tight and the prospect of making a start in the garden was still someway off. Nevertheless, in my mind's eye I could see the sort of thing I wanted and could even visualize the part of our garden that I thought most suitable, so out came the measuring tape and dimensions were noted. Notice that I say

Left: The halt at Bittner Moor basks in the warmth of a sultry summer afternoon as the local goods trundles gently past the rocky outcrops, where thymes cling tenaciously by thrusting roots into cracks and fissures and the more verdant ground covers creep towards the track.

Right: The permanent-way gang are overdue, judging by the state of some of the rail spikes as a selection of home-built stock rolls past tree-like *Lonicera nitidia* and onward through the aromatic mounds of *Thymus Silver Posie.*

Lower: The brake van is a variation on the theme of box modelling, dimensions being similar to other North Lindsey vans but having the luxury of a veranda where the incumbent guard is able to while away many a pleasant hour in nostalgic reverie of his former quasi-military existence.

our garden - very important to get the family on side, as things are much easier if you can harness the combined enthusiasm of the household.

A Likely Evolution

Most gardens have a likely evolution too, so that the sand pit and swing that once seemed so important to junior family members can probably be re-located or disappear altogether as you plan for the garden to incorporate a railway. I tried hard to foster the interest that my partner was already showing in matters horti-cultural, so there was no hardship in nurturing her enthusiasm for a miniature landscape which I hoped would set the ambience for the line and be an essential part of the whole railway atmos-phere. Not only did I want to operate trains, I wanted them to be a visually acceptable part of the setting, rather than an intrusion into an existing twelve inches to the foot world, where daffodils, tulips, roses and other plants, might tower awkwardly over the track and rolling stock like giants from an alien world. The landscape I envisaged would be planted with small leaved shrub varieties and dwarf tree stock that would be specially chosen to lend credence to the image of the narrow gauge in harmony with the garden - though, where do you begin when most of your gardening experience consists of growing a few vegetables and the weekly cutting and tidying of grass? I made a move in the direction of my local library and searched for books on rock gardening and miniature planting, dipping into them often to acquaint myself with information that might be needed in our quest to provide the railway with the preferred backdrop. Nurseries, I decided, had much more specialist knowledge than garden centres and I was able to see and investigate small-leaved

plant varieties to discover what conditions they preferred; whether ground covering or upright in their habit; their growth rates and likely sizes after ten years. Eventually I was able to muster the courage to make a reasonably informed choice and start planting on the emerging, but bare earthworks of the North Lindsey Light Railway.

Just how much space can realistically be allocated to your garden railway scheme depends on your circumstances, but gaining an intimate knowledge of the dimensions involved helped me to convert the proposed track plans sketched on the backs of large envelopes into a dependable scale plan from which I've hardly deviated since the first spadeful of earth was moved. It's important to know, even at this stage, whether the layout you want will be out & back, end-to-end, continuous run

Left: Douglas George, the Accucraft *'Caradoc'* loco, makes light work of the gradient up to and over the viaduct, the concrete sections of which can be discerned. The normal scale garden in the distance by the wall is far enough away at this point not to make a negative impact on the miniature planting that had been started in this winter view, although there is an abundance of bare earth to be planted in the spring.

Lower: Visitors to the railway have noticed a striking similarity between Ken, the Lister driver and Ewan who drives *Frances*, the kit-built Roundhouse 0-6-0 tank loco. The truth is that they are from the same family - out of the same mould, you might say, but Ewan is firmly wedded to steam traction and wearing his overalls, jacket and grease top cap, always drives Frances.

all, nothing succeeds like success - or you can wade in regardless of others and learn from your own mistakes. There is a middle road, which is probably the one that most of us decide to take since the combination of our gardens; our resources, our circumstances and our physical capabilities are unlike those of anyone else. Besides, we're individuals with ideas that we like to think of as our own and we want to test them and try them out and sometimes push our imaginations to the limit, regardless of the practicalities involved. It was this stubbornness that caused me to become involved with steel fabrications and welding, as I perceived that this was the best method of building a secure foundation for the track on graded sections of line. Level sections were blocks on a substantial concrete footing, as I wanted minimal movement and I feel vindicated in having worked out my solution to this particular challenge, for with soil settlement over the last few years, inevitably, the landscape has moved, but the foundation, upon which the track is established, has not. There is a price to pay which, in my case was lots of hard physical labour, but you have to work out the 'cost' and decide whether it's worth it. However, if there's a chance that you may be moving house on a regular basis, perhaps this sort of permanent construction is of limited value and there is clearly a great deal going for the easily dismantled wooden structures that form the basis of so many splendid garden railways.

I was keen to get started on my new project in the garden but tried to keep a sense of proportion related to what little cash I could spare, so realistically set myself a time target to attain the status of 'up & running'. Two years sounds an eternity in an age when many want an 'instant railway', but I was prepared to set realistic targets and work steadily towards making the best foundation that I could for a venture that I viewed as long term. This involved spending money on some pretty basic stuff, like steel, crushed limestone and concrete, when I would rather have been considering track, rolling stock or locos but common sense tells you that effort and resources are best invested in the basics and, in any case, I had made some useful contacts for the

or various permutations of these. Using a copy of the track plan, I even constructed a three dimensional model using card and balsa, which helped me think my way around the gradients and associated 'cut & fill' that would be needed later when I put on my railway navvy's cap. Of course, I could have avoided much of this hard work if only I'd planned for tracks to be level, but that option wouldn't have been so interesting or as much fun either then, when I was a railway navvy, or later when I'd been promoted to engine driver and was enjoying the challenge of trying to keep to a scale 15 mph up-hill and down-dale!

'Up and Running' Status

You can weigh the advice given by those who have experience of garden railways and try to avoid some of the pitfalls - after

Roj is a rugged little Lister built from an IP Engineering kit with the addition of a heavily modified Star Wars model figure and is powered by a couple of AA rechargeable batteries. When coupled to the flat wagon with fuel tank, scratch built, literally, from odds and ends, the scene is evocative of such locos operating at quarries and industrial works throughout the land.

supply of recycled materials that helped me keep well within my budget, not least of which was the gift of about ten tons of spoil from a neighbours driveway - all I had to do was barrow it to my embankments! More came from a friend who was demolishing a building and gave me all the hardcore I wanted, which I buried under my own good topsoil. All this 'free stuff' came at the cost of my own labour - acceptable for the long-term gains it offered!

Meanwhile, the acquisition of some ancient O-gauge track parts guided me to investigate the possibility of making my own track. There are several factors to be taken into account, not least of which is the eternal question of money, but for many there's also a shortage of available time, so in the end, it's a balancing act and the individual makes a decision to buy ready made track or DIY, based purely on circumstances. I'm very happy with my low cost, home-grown track, the rails of which are spiked to deep wooden sleepers that float in a substantial ballast and behave in a most prototypical railway manner, even down to the faint odour of creosote on hot summer afternoons, a poignant evocation of youthful days spent around my local, but long departed railway.

Constantly Evolving Landscape

Our railway was named after the local standard gauge line, remnants of which still survive, and the North Lindsey Light Railway exists in 16mm narrow gauge form in its own parallel universe within our garden, having grown from bare mounds of earth to a mature but constantly evolving landscape over the last few years. I'd wanted a controllable steam loco from the time when, back in the 1980s, I allowed myself the luxury of a Mamod live steamer that the children and I would watch as it thrashed round an oval of track set out in the garden on sunny afternoons. I eventually bought a kit of parts for a '*Lady Anne*' 0-6-0 tank loco from Roundhouse Engineering, which has made up into a commendably inexpensive 'quality' loco. *Frances* operated for little more than a season under manual control, after which I converted her to radio control due to the gradients on the line. I have to say that, had I made the NLLR level throughout, *Frances* would still be running as built, being easily controlled on the level but the graded line does require steam locos to be driven and radio control certainly does help to achieve that as the regulator can be adjusted without having to chase the loco around the track. Battery electric locos

and railcars, however, generally take the gradients in their stride, though this depends upon loadings and how much work you give them to do and assumes that the batteries are in the best of health.

Roj is a rugged little Lister built from an IP Engineering kit with the addition of a heavily modified *Star Wars* model figure and is powered by a couple of AA rechargeable batteries. When coupled to the flat wagon with fuel tank, scratch built, literally, from odds and ends, the scene is evocative of such locos operating at quarries and industrial works throughout the land. The *Star Wars* figure was a sale item at 50p from a local supermarket and Obi-Wan-Kenobi submitted without a murmur to the surgeon's knife in the quest to lead a more useful existence as driver/handyman Ken on the NLLR! There are some beautifully modelled scale figures for garden railways available from the trade, which represent good value when you consider the effort that goes into their manufacture. Nonetheless, their cost can be very high if you are populating your scenes in significant numbers and a cheaper alternative, if you have the time and inclination is to make your own from scratch or modify the mass-produced figures often to be found very cheaply in 'bargain' shops. Ordinary modelling tools, such as a craft knife and razor saw, with epoxy glue and car body filler are the stock in trade of the would be plastic surgeon. Not only should we remember that humans come in a huge variety of shapes and sizes and therefore there is no 'correct' size for your scale, but that a suggestion of character, perhaps in the demeanour or attitude, is as good as a finely detailed moulding since we are not generally viewing from very close quarters.

Sometimes it is highly appropriate to model caricatures, which can be taken to extremes, if you so wish!

You're Making a Simple Box

Since her conversion to radio control, *Frances* is a powerful and easy to handle locomotive limited in her adhesion on the gradients only by the load she's hauling and the amount of moisture on the railheads. If you try to overdo things, she's inclined to slip and spin her small wheels producing rather spectacular amounts of exhaust steam, so it is best to proceed with caution when opening the regulator. *Frances* shares the heavier workings with 0-4-0-tank engine, *Douglas George,* a quality loco from the Accucraft range at a budget price. This loco was rather swiftly converted to radio control to make it easier to handle on the gradients and has proved to be a capable performer. Both engines handle passenger and goods stock in equal measure and because rolling stock is homemade from recycled wood, there is plenty of mass for them both to cope with. The recycling of materials is a recurring theme on the NLLR; putting to good use resources that would otherwise have finished up in the skip, adding to the nations ever growing waste problem - not that even the most determined effort on the part of garden railers is going to make any difference there. From my perspective, though, it makes sense to utilise second-hand materials where possible and use cash for bits and pieces you can't easily make. Apparently, I've been well tarred with the brush that was immersed in the 'make do and mend' culture of yesteryear and though I'm not suggesting that we all immediately

Left: When the continuous run had been completed Frances was steamed for the first time and we celebrated by attaching all our rolling stock - the converted G-scale Bachmann coach!

Right: The unique Mercedes motor van, *Ramblin' Mally*, named after a loquacious friend and manned by his 16mm doppelganger gathers speed as it leaves the tunnel and heads for Hudson's Bank with a short train of small vehicles. The rocky terrain at this point is gradually being softened by the creeping ground cover, *Herniaria glabra*, or rupture wort, as it is otherwise known.

Lower: Inspired by the railcars from over the water in County Donegal, this articulated railcar recently entered service on the North Lindsey Light Railway and, apart from the motor and radio-control equipment, has been made principally from recycled materials. Definitely not a box modelling project and though I've had to pause for thought now and then, a sense of achievement followed its building.

adopt this outlook, if you happen to find it difficult to justify the sort of expenditure necessary to furnish your railway with ready to run equipment, you might care to explore a more hands on, DIY approach. For some, this can be challenging but perseverance brings manifold rewards.

Making your own wagons and vans, for example, is not as difficult as it might at first seem and if you really are not sure where to start, then how about tackling a kit of parts just to get the feel of it. It's probably well worth the modest outlay and there are several firms who offer rolling stock parts, including pre-cut and scribed wagon sides that, essentially just need gluing carefully together after you've checked for squareness and done a little rubbing down with fine glass paper. Fundamentally, you're making a simple box and once you've digested the idea

there's nothing to stop you building variations on a theme - after all, a van is only a wagon with a roof! White metal castings are available for axle boxes or how about the excellent plastic injection mouldings that are available. If you use brass bearings to suit the chosen wheel journal diameter, with a drop of light oil, they'll last for years. My goods rolling stock, with one exception have been built from scrap wood and ply to a basic and uncomplicated design with variations in dimensions to give variety when vehicles are marshalled together. Little by little I get around to adding very simple detailing, but much of the North Lindsey stock is of an elementary nature and when it's on the move, super-detailing is much less noticeable. Perhaps it is worthwhile, however, to give extra attention to the last vehicle in the rake, like fixing a red lamp on the buffer beam of the guards

Left: **In a glow of summer colour, Ewan drives his train steadily over the viaduct and will be preparing to close the regulator and drift gently down the grade to the halt at Bittner Moor, where there may be passengers to pick up, by request.**

Lower: **The rustic peace at Bittner Moor is disturbed for a few moments as *Ramblin Mally* saunters into the tunnel with a few empties. The shelter and small office have been constructed using rudiments adapted from wagon building with scribed plywood pieces glued together to form the basic box shape, the frame of the structure and other trappings being added later. The store shed next to the office represents a redundant railway van; again straightforward box modelling embellished with simple features, including the baked bean tin corrugated iron roof.**

van or posing the guard as if looking out from the veranda, as this is the wagon that eyes may follow after the passing of a train.

There are few buildings on the narrow gauge North Lindsey at present but the little wooden shelter and ticket office at Bittner Moor Junction have set the style for buildings that will surely follow. Surprising as it might seem, the rudiments are adapted from wagon building with scribed plywood pieces glued together to form the basic box shape, the 'frame' of the structure and other trappings being added later. The store shed next to the office represents a redundant railway van; again straightforward 'box' modelling embellished with simple features, including the baked bean tin 'corrugated iron' roof.

Chiefly Recycled Materials

Other structures on the line include the bridges, which represent a variety of types, all adding interest to the scene, all built from

recycled materials with only the viaduct costing more than a couple of day's work. The viaduct was made from parts cast in two simple wooden moulds that I knocked up from scraps of exterior grade plywood, whilst steel plate from an old fuel tank was used to manufacture two of the bridges and a redundant bed frame donated parts for the arched bridge over the ravine, the curves being hammered into cold steel one afternoon when I felt the need to release a little tension! Granted, you may need access to a welding set or an electric drill and some 'pop' rivets as an alternative means of fixing bits of steel together, but this is where the garden rail fraternity may prove useful as we all have our own strengths and skills, which can be traded with others so that we get things done!

Powered rolling stock has been built and added to the collection of vehicles that can be rostered to provide an intriguing selection of narrow gauge transport for the delight of the visitor. All these models have been built at home using chiefly recycled materials, apart from motor and control equipment, and take their inspiration from actual railways. They are not built as scale replicas and the resultant prototypes owe more to whimsical supposition and a desire to make something unique for the North Lindsey.

Since being established in the early days of the new millennium, the North Lindsey Light Railway has operated successfully and has been a source of enjoyment for hundreds of invited guests who generously donate funds for a chosen charity on the occasion of our 'Midsummer Night Steam'. For most visitors, the appeal seems to be in the overall feeling of the railway - the ambience created by the aesthetic juxtaposition of engineering and setting; in other words, the placing of the railway into a miniature landscape, which is believable because it is the sum of all its parts. It is far from being finished and, due to its continuing evolution is unlikely ever to reach that stage when we can down tools and call it a day.

Main Line Magnificence

Nowadays the larger proportion of garden railways tend to be of a narrow gauge format, using either 16mm scale or G-scale equipment. Now this is fine if you like either bucolic little locomotives running at ten miles an hour with short and often fairly decrepit trains - or the colourful and efficient electrically powered Continental metre gauge railways. If however, your heart is stirred by memories of the ACE running hard to the West, or perhaps by the florid beauty of standard gauge trains in the Edwardian era, then Gauge One will be able to provide all this and more, using live steam, battery or track power.

Barry Pulford was born in Worthing in 1936. After leaving school in 1952, he completed an engineering apprenticeship with the de Havilland Aircraft Company and worked in the aerodynamics office. He later moved to the Atomic Energy Authority and the Central Electricity Generating Board working as a professional engineer in research.

A lifelong interest in railways was concentrated on live steam models by a visit to the Brighton Toy Museum in 1998 where he first saw, smelt and heard, Bowman steam trains in action. Now retired, he tells me that he is trying to recover the basic workshop skills that mostly eluded him during those early years in order to enjoy his hobby. A regular contributor to *GardenRail* magazine, Barry likes to keep the standard gauge flag flying with his photographs of both fine scale and vintage Gauge One in action...

Aster No.4472 *'Flying Scotsman'*, a three-cylinder loco with working conjugated valves, is seen passing through a country station at ground level on the Walnut Tree Line. The teak coaches are hand built to 1/32 scale to match the loco. The couple on the bench don't seem that impressed - perhaps they have other fish to fry...

Model railway track was first standardised into gauges by Märklin when he showed his new train lines at the Leipzig Fair in 1891. The gauge was measured from centre to centre of the rails and the then smallest, 48mm, was given the number 1. All his gauges used a rounded railhead of 3mm diameter so the actual distance between rails was 3mm less than the nominal dimension, resulting in 45mm for Gauge One. The standard railway gauge is 4ft-8½ins, which for Gauge One is now represented in Britain by a track gauge of 1¾ins (approximately 45mm) with the trains running on it made to a

A view of the Highland Railway inspired Findhorn Railway. Heathers are much in evidence providing mature and appropriate scenery. 0-6-0 HR Class 'K' or *'Drummond Goods'* No 135 comes round the loop, showing the interest that can be achieved even in a short goods train, as a *'Skye Bogie'* with its train waits in the station. It would seem that the local track gang have been at work on the platform road in recent days.

scale of 10mm to the foot, giving a scale ratio of 1:30.5. Germany and the USA use the same track gauge with the trains made to a scale of ⅜ins to the foot, giving a scale ratio of 1:32. Aster Hobbies Ltd, a major supplier of Gauge One locos, also use this scale. Which scale you choose is a matter of personal preference. With a scale of ⅜ins to the foot the train is the same scale as the track, whilst with 10mm to the foot the trains are slightly larger. In practice this means less than ¼in on the height of an average loco. Mixing the two scales is not unacceptable, but preferably not in the same train.

The Gauge One Model Railway Association (G1MRA) was formed around 1947 and now has just over 1900 members worldwide. Its objects include the promotion of railway modelling in Gauge One, bringing together persons interested in the construction of Gauge One models and organizing meetings for running them.

Gauge One trains comprising an express passenger locomotive hauling a representative rake of bogie coaches will need some-

Right: **Drummond Goods rolling majestically across the viaduct on the Findhorn Railway. This superb structure was constructed using hundreds of individual pieces of broken roofing tile. It has only recently been built and will no doubt look even better when weathered.**

Lower: **Live Steam Midland Compound No 1000 emerges into the autumn sunshine, the oily streaks on the boiler giving indication of an overactive lubricator.**

Lower left: **An Aster** *'King Arthur'* **Class** *Sir Galleron* **has been rebuilt with a fire tube boiler replacing the original Smithies type. Among other advantages this is kinder on the boiler paintwork.**

thing like 10ft radius and therefore a correspondingly large space. However, you may wish to model something more modest; the railways of the Isle of Wight for example employed small tank engines with, in the early days, four wheeled coaches that would run on a smaller garden railway. Similarly those wishing to run historic trains such as the Aster *'Lion'* or *'Titfield Thunderbolt'* with period rolling stock will not need the larger radius curves. Or you could have an end-to-end track representing a branch line of which there were, and probably still are, many full size examples.

Sidings and Passing Loops

Many Gauge One modellers have a strong interest in building locomotives and treat their railway more as a test track or running facility than a fully developed scenic one. These railways are quite often simply a well built oval of track mounted on an elevated base with either no scenery at all, or just a limited number of portable buildings such as stations, signal boxes and one or more lifting bridges providing access to the inside of the tracks. However, this type of railway may be developed into a part scenic layout by building walls under some of the track, or planting suitable shrubs to fill the space under the boards and provide scenic edging.

Some of these include impressive structures such as viaducts, or where there is an American influence, trestle bridges. Another approach is to create a ground level railway, and this can be very realistic in Gauge One, with embankments, shallow cuttings and even a tunnel, provided it is not too long. The often-stated disadvantage with ground level railways is the

difficulty in reaching the locomotive controls. This is certainly the case with manually operated live steam locos run by the maturely challenged! Radio control is a possible answer.

If you are fortunate enough to have a garden on sloping ground, or with variations in level of around two to three feet it is possible to have a part ground level scenic railway with another part of it at a convenient height, say between two to three feet, for locomotive preparation and operating requirements like adding water and fuel.

A further consideration when contemplating a garden railway in Gauge One is whether or not one wishes to enter into the full

'*Skye Bogie*' No 70 crosses a bridge on the Findhorn Railway with a Highland Railway train. Note the passenger communication alarm bell on the tender side. The leading vehicle is a Drummond six wheel brake.

social side catered for by G1MRA who have, in recent years, encouraged the establishment of area groups. Some members of the group who have a garden railway open them to fellow members of the group once or twice a year. Should you wish to construct a garden railway with a view to holding 'get-togethers' you might consider the number of people you want to attend, and provide adequate space for locos to be steamed up in preparation for running and for cooling down afterwards. This usually takes the form of sidings and passing loops, although you could have carriage sidings and a comprehensive motive power depot complete with turntable. The choice is yours but never forget the all-important negotiations with and planning approval from other garden users in the family. The best advice that I received regarding the type of garden railway to build was, "Seek advice by all means, but at the end of the day you must decide what you want to do and do it."

Märklin, Bing and Carrette

The early Gauge One trains were usually powered by clock-work mechanisms, some with braking and reversing operated

Right: Aster *'Schools'* Class No.919 *Harrow* passes the old Water Mill on the Ford Line. This loco has been rebuilt with beam compensated driving wheels and a fire tube boiler.

Lower: An artist is seen here at work, feeding coal onto the miniature grate of his live steam Midland 4F, which with BR coaches, is running on a very sturdy railway.

Lower left: A period train comprising an LNWR loco and oil-lit 4-wheelers passing through mature scenery on an elevated railway.

by levers in the cab, or by live steam and later, as it became available in peoples homes, electricity. Gauge One clockwork trains were popular in the early 1900s, most of those available in Britain being made by German manufacturers such as Märklin, Bing and Carrette, and sold through Gamages or Bassett-Lowke. However, after the First World War, 1914-18, there was resistance from the British public to buying products from Germany. Also, although some Gauge One products continued, by the 1930s they were being replaced more and more by Gauge 0 trains made by Hornby and others. With the gradual move to the smaller gauges clockwork Gauge One trains became less popular until today when they are mostly the province of collectors and operators of vintage trains. Clockwork trains still have a fascination of their own, being very 'hands on'. For example, on a railway with intermediate stations trains can be operated, with practice, to just reach the next station stop before having to be rewound.

In Britain live steam began with rather primitive engines known as dribblers for reasons that may be imagined. At first these ran directly on the floor but later on tracks, including Gauge One. At the same time, much as with clockwork trains, foreign and British manufacturers were supplying more sophisticated models recognizable as small editions of real life prototypes. Starting in the 1920s there was growing interest in model making as a hobby and amateur steam engine makers were encouraged by writers like Lillian 'Curly' Laurence, writing under the pen name L.B.S.C. in the Model Engineer, to make their own steam engines. They were supported by a growing industry of small manufacturers supplying castings and specialized components,

some of which progressed to making complete locos. This is very much the situation today where small companies provide ready to run live steam Gauge One locos and rolling stock, or kits of parts for home construction. Live steam locos may be coal fired, using coal or charcoal, spirit fired using methylated spirits or gas fired using butane. Whichever fuel you use for live steam you will be reminded of the wonderful aura of wellbeing and warmth associated with the real thing.

Great Western No 619 *King Charles II* was built in 1947 for Captain Warrell for use on his Magna Charta line where it was reputed to have hauled fifty carriages. It was originally electrically powered with stud contact. The model was supposed to be weighted with lead to assist adhesion but, on converting to battery power, the present owner found it was filled with tintacks and putty.

On Board Battery Power

The first electrically powered locos were models of real electric locos as running on French or Swiss railways. The current was supplied from accumulators or from the domestic supply, usually transformed to a lower voltage for safety, and picked up by a collector under the loco from a third rail or studs between the running tracks. As the convenience and remote control benefit of electric power was recognized it spread to models of steam outline prototypes. Improvements in electric motor design and miniaturization greatly influenced the popularity of the smaller gauges, whilst the desire for realism led to a return to two-rail operation. Electric power in the garden with pickup from the track, or even overhead catenaries, is possible provided due consideration is given to safety, but not much used for Gauge One these days.

The alternative, becoming popular with improvements in electric motor efficiency and battery technology, is the use of on-board battery power with a speed controller operated manually or by radio control. Electric or battery power, although also convenient for steam outline, is particularly suited to electric or diesel locos and railcars.

A brief word on radio control; some proponents believe that all locos in the garden should be radio controlled, others, some

Right: **Scratch-built Adams L.S.W.R. Class 0415 No 3125 as running in SR days with a rake of ex South Western coaches. The train is passing through some spectacular scenery on the Walnut Tree Line.**

Lower: **Southern 2BIL with on-board battery power and radio controlled speed controller. Electro Motive Units (EMUs) are well suited to an 'end to end' line.**

Lower left: **No 70 is seen here in charge of a train of Highland Railway coaches waiting at the intermediate station which provides a passing loop on the otherwise single track Findhorn Railway.**

live steam operators among them, prefer manual control. My own observation is that many users of radio control spend more time running round with their train than those without radio! However, it is very popular and an area you may wish to try for yourself. But remember it is not obligatory and the skilful manual operation of regulator and blower or gas valve is very satisfying.

Acquiring suitable rolling stock for Gauge One trains can be expensive; a ten coach or forty wagon train costing more than a loco. However there are many prototypical examples of trains suitable for the garden of more manageable size. If one is modelling a period of time gone by, as many of us do, then short mixed goods trains and two or three coach branch trains are very acceptable. There are a number of suppliers of passenger coaches of all types together with goods trucks, vans and so on both in kit form and ready to run. Equally one can purchase wheels, buffers and couplings and other parts to aid scratch building. As with all aspects of modelling the level of detail you incorporate is up to you, there are no hard and fast rules. If you have spent thousands of pounds on, or years of your life making a museum quality model you are hardly likely to risk it at sixty miles an hour in the garden - or are you?

Pass Through the Countryside

Gardening, love it or hate it, will grow on you once you build your railway. Real railways run through real towns and real countryside. It may be observed that whereas indoor model railways often run through model towns filled with houses and factories, garden railways pass through the countryside as represented by natural vegetation. This can be enhanced by taking advantage of natural features and by careful choice of planting. If the railway, or part of it, is at ground level the grass will represent open fields with small shrubs appearing as woodland areas, or a pond a lake. Where we choose to have the railway elevated it

Left: **'Skye Bogie' No 70 ready to depart past the wooden signal box and stone built water tower. Look at the detailed cab interior on this locomotive.**

Centre: **A Southern Railway 'Battle of Britain' Class 21C167 Tangmere with Bulleid coaches in malachite green. The loco is electrically powered using rechargeable batteries with a radio controlled speed controller.**

Lower: **Waiting for its next turn of duty, Southern E4 No.2507 relaxes on the Wealden Line showing no sign of pressure at all.**

may be possible to take advantage of a wall or bank. If not, and it becomes necessary to create an elevated structure, then the space between the ground and the track level can be filled with hedging, shrubs or heather, preferably evergreen. If allowed to grow to different levels this will give the impression of the railway passing through undulating ground with cuttings and embankments. We are not all gardeners but perhaps our partners are, so seek their advice in selecting, planting and maintaining this most important visual aspect of the garden railway.

Where the railway crosses a garden path or other essential right of way for access to a shed, greenhouse, washing line or whatever, one can build in a removable, lifting or swinging section. And if you wish to show off your civil engineering skills, disguise it as a bridge, arch, viaduct or whatever. The only limit is your imagination.

With a whisper of steam for pardon,
The squeal of the wheels for mirth,
Gauge One is better in a garden,
Than anywhere else on earth.
(With apologies to Dorothy Frances Gurney)

The Russet Tor Light Railway

There are all sorts of different ways of entering the world of garden railways. *Phil Sixsmith* has been interested in model making for as long as he can remember, progressing from Airfix kits as a youngster to scratch building today. Phil, like myself, made the move from N-gauge modelling to large-scale stuff in the garden - although in my case, I was very much an 'armchair-modeller', with little more than a collection of N-gauge locomotives and rolling stock.

The Russet Tor Light Railway is what the indoor scales call a 'freelance' model, this line being 'its own prototype' and this is very much an ethos that I feel at home with. Phil is a keen gardener and how the garden fits with the railway he feels, is far more important than the right number of rivets on the tender. I am told that the narrow gauge inspiration for this line is the Lynton and Barnstable Railway and hopefully, in the not too distant future, we will all be able to take a train from a revitalised Woody Bay station through the stunning North Devon scenery.

Perhaps it is the attraction of the tiny and self-contained, the small-scale world in the back garden that works the way we want it to! It does not matter what others feel is right. Phil puts it thus, "My lovely wife leaves me to my own little world and the girls have long since gotten over being vaguely interested in any of my garden railway projects..."

Be that as it may, the delightful narrow gauge railway empire constructed by *Phil Sixsmith* has atmosphere and style in spades. Enjoy, with me, the inspirational photographs...

My particular adventure into the world of garden railways started with a dramatic change of scale from an N-gauge layout of a main line set in 50/60s Britain to a 16mm scale idyllic narrow gauge preserved railway in the garden...

The seed of the idea had been sown at our eldest daughters 2nd birthday party on a warm day in May, 1990. To entertain the assembled guests, visiting dignitaries from the already established Little Angel Light Railway brought along a circle of LGB first radius track and two locomotives - one battery powered and the other a live steam Merlin *'Monarch'*. At the end of the day's festivities, the locos returned home but the track was donated to the newly formed Russet Tor Preservation Society and, over the past fifteen years, the railway has grown from those small beginnings into a continuous run around the confines of our small suburban garden.

In fact when I set out to build a railway in the garden, I knew very little about narrow gauge railways. For me it was simply the

chance to model on a bigger scale. Nowadays, whenever I see N-gauge layouts at exhibitions, I really cannot believe how small it is!

Whilst many people have created their 16mm railways to represent a true prototype, others, like myself, have opted for the freelance approach and the Russet Tor Light Railway is very much its own prototype. Certainly I can see the attraction of the prototypical modelling, but I do feel that our scale lends itself equally well to the freelance modeller. After all, many a narrow gauge line in the 12ins to the foot world bought in their motive power from the same manufacturer who provided locomotives for other railways - but still retained their own character and identity. Similarly the Roundhouse locomotives running on our line belong to our railway. The Russet Tor has its own identity; its own history, traditions and aspirations.

A Genuine Escape

Garden railways are a long-term project that will develop and mature with you over time. The Russet Tor has become for me a very real place. I can visit anytime and it's a genuine escape from the pressures of everyday life beyond the garden fence. Even when there are no trains running, be it in the depths of winter or on a summer's morning, when I draw back the curtains from the dining room widow and look out and catch a glimpse of Allington Station, it is enough to get the day off to a good start - and if the day doesn't pan out as I had planned, I can always come home and 'set fire' to a loco for a run into the sunset to help me unwind.

Allington is the railway's 'main' station and has a small goods shed. Bramley Halt is the line's other stopping point but passengers using this facility can expect a fair old walk to the village of Bramley. There are plans to bring at least parts of the village to within sight of the station but that's an example of one of those long-term aspirations! Until then perhaps I should rename the station 'Bramley Road' as the great Western

Devon, in repainted blue livery with her tender pause at Allington signal box awaiting the all clear. Although manually controlled, the first coach conceals a governor mechanism built by David Wilding with parts liberated from an old dial-operated telephone. This was commissioned as the solution to prevent *Devon* from running away on the one and only downgrade on the Russet Tor. The faster she tries to go the harder the governor works to hold her back. The results have been better than I could ever have wished. With the regulator half open she trundles round at a constant slow speed. Dave has subsequently fitted a chuff pipe and as the loco has to pull against the governor she makes a satisfying rasping exhaust.

That glimpse through the dining room window that can raise a smile on any day. There may be no trains running but the railway still looks good! A single van waits at the goods shed for collection. A brake van sits in the bay platform. You get the feeling that a train could be due at any time! I like to leave one or two items of stock out at all times, after all this is a real railway and how many stations have you ever visited where there are not one or two wagons hanging around for collection? Both vans are scratch built Plasticard efforts on Playmobile wheel sets. The goods shed is based on a standard gauge prototype and is Plasticard planks on a timber frame.

Railway used to do when their stations were situated a long way from the settlement they purported to serve.

Just down the line from Allington are the loco servicing facilities, consisting of a small engine shed, water tower, coal dump and turntable. In truth I never thought the railway would ever have more than one live steamer but, over the years, the loco fleet has steadily grown to four 'living' engines. In the early days the link with the Little Angel Light Railway ensured that live steam was a frequent weekend attraction on the fledgling railway

Passenger numbers on these weekend specials were always high. Clearly the way forward was for the Russet Tor to have its own live steam attraction. This was a major commitment for the preservation team to take on, but with the long-term future of the line in mind, funds were raised and in 1992 an order placed with the Merlin Locomotive Works for a gas-fired, radio controlled *'Mayflower'*.

Whistles and Draincocks

The loco duly arrived in July of the same year and entered service as *Emma*, named after our eldest daughter. After all it had been the entertainment at her party two years earlier that had been one of the main inspirations for the Russet Tor's revival. *Rachel*, a magnificent Roundhouse *'Russell'* class 2-6-2, also joined the Russet Tor shed in 2000. *Rachel* is now a very impressive performer, having had a whistle and working drain cock effect, retro fitted by the very talented John Fox. Named after our other daughter, she was an instant success, providing the reliability and slow running performance that the Merlin sadly lacked.

The Merlin was however much improved with the aid of Tag Gorton who provided at very reasonable cost, a set of much

Above: Bryn seemed an apt name for my Glyn Valley inspired tram engine, scratch built around a Playmobile chassis block, seen here basking in the sunlight after a turn of duty on the Russet Tor. Her fireman is more intent on getting his vintage Triumph to start for the journey home rather than polishing his engine.

Right: A busy day at Allington goods shed, the maintenance team are repainting some of the weatherboarding, whilst the bearded ex sailor waits for the transport to unload his new boat which has arrived ahead of schedule. Our intrepid motorcyclist is still having trouble with his bike! The goods shed is based on a standard gauge prototype and is Plasticard planks on a timber frame.

Lower: 'Lyn', converted to an on board battery powered loco; she is lightly used, lacking the pulling power of the other battery locos in the fleet. Bob, one of the Russet Tor senior drivers has an easy job shovelling out the 7.2volt ash from the smoke box! One of the younger firemen, who were formally employed as one of the Tamiya racing pit team, is more intent on tinkering with his very unreliable Triumph motorcycle.

needed machined brass piston heads with proper 'o' ring seals to replace the original and now failing Beck plastic originals. Further improvement was achieved in 2004 with the fitting of a 40meg FM radio control set and the excellent SM32 replacement valve chests from Milton Locomotive Works. *Emma* will

Left: Devon running over Accuba Bridge with a rake of four-wheelers. The farmer's children tending to their animals under the bridge are Early Learning Centre issue. The bridge is plywood covered with individual Plasticard stonework. The bridge deck is a length of redundant electrical conduit tray.

Right: Devon being prepared for the afternoon train. The crew are a combination of the much-used early Learning Centre farmer, promoted to engine driver and a member of the cast from Jurassic Park 3. I think it's Sam Neil, a Hollywood star happily working for free on the RT. The engine shed is plywood with painted on stone effect. The doors are Plasticard on working strap hinges, hung on bent panel pins.

never be as good as the Roundhouse locos in the fleet, but she has always been admired for her good looks and is now able to easily hold her own on a passenger service and is enjoying a second lease of life.

The other two live steamers are also Roundhouse. A manual *'Bertie'* class loco *Devon*, repainted and provided with a tender and a *'Millie'*, *Jenny Wrenn*. Originally owned and extensively altered and improved by John Fox, she ran on the now sadly closed Foxfield Light Railway. *'Millie'* is however 32mm gauge and currently is only available for running at other lines of fellow members of the 16mm society.

The long-term plan is to lay a 32mm branch line for *Jenny Wrenn* and other 32mm stock but that's another aspiration and, hopefully, another chapter in the history of the Russet Tor.

In truth the lines first steamer was technically a Mamod, donated by the Little Angel Light Railway, but the Mamod loco was not however as great a success. Like many before and I suspect many in the future, I found that to get it to run at all was, to say the least, a challenge. When it did go it only ran as far as the first curve and at a scale speed approaching the sound barrier. The result was that it left the rails with annoying regularity. Despite efforts to tame the beast with various add on improvements the decision was made to cut my losses and the loco was withdrawn from service. My Mamod never actually pulled a service train - but don't let my experience put you off. Over the years I have seen many a Mamod doing sterling work on other peoples lines.

Wickham Works Trolley

A battery powered Glyn Valley inspired tram engine, *Bryn*, a single Fairlie *Berwyn Belle* and an Irish inspired railcar, all built by the RT workshops, compliment the live steam locos, while a Bachmann *'Lyn'*, converted to battery-powered operation,

Right: A *GardenRail* magazine reader relaxes at Allington before boarding his train of *Bryn* pulling two repainted LGB four wheel Zillerbahn coaches with a Ffestiniog inspired brake combine built around a much altered Bachmann G-scale passenger car.

Lower: Captain Nesbit is a frequent user of the line. A keen golfer in his retirement years he prefers the comfort of travelling on the lines Irish inspired railcar. I can't recall the name of the trader but the Captain was one of a range of highly detailed, unpainted, resin cast figures on sale at one of the Llanfair GardenRail shows. The Irish railcar is another of the lines motive power fleet built utilising the very useful Playmobile chassis. The body is Plasticard with a shaped balsa roof. The headlamp came from a local shop that specialised in maritime modelling.

completes the main motive power. Recently we have added an IP Engineering *'Lister'* and also a Wickham inspired works trolley, originally built on a motor block liberated from an ASDA toy truck, but now running on an IP Engineering budget chassis.

Until last season most of the passenger stock was scratch built or converted Bachmann coaches, but these have been gradually replaced with coaches produced by two other members of our group, David and Mathew Wilding. David has a deserved reputation for his skills as an engineer and innovator. The coaches are made of hardboard, with recessed panels and window openings cut and machined utilising a computer programme written by the

Left: Roundhouse *'Russell'* class loco *Rachel*, named after our youngest daughter makes an impressive arrival at Allington shrouded in steam. The steam effects are thanks to fellow 16miller John Fox whose masterpiece of a three way valve gives the choice of drain cocks effects, whistle or chimney exhaust, all via radio control.

Lower: With safety valve lifting, during the prolonged station stop, *Rachel* waits impatiently for the Guards signal.

man himself in his own lean-to workshop. Sadly these coaches are limited edition runs and myself, with a few other lucky owners, feel very grateful to them both for the time they have invested to produce them.

For most of its existence, the Russet Tor Light Railway has only been known to a few like-minded modellers and friends, but in 2000, via a message posted on a 16mm egroup, I made contact with Chris MacKenzie, a member of the 16mm Association who lived locally. At the time I was contemplating rejoining the Association although I admit I had some reservations. From the outside the Association gave me the impression that they were a group of narrow gauge enthusiasts who exclusively modelled two-foot prototypes. I had been a member, albeit for

only twelve months, some ten years earlier. At that time I was just beginning in the garden and I was a little overwhelmed at what appeared in the magazine.

I attended only one garden meet with a fellow modeller who also ran on 45mm track. We each took along a radio controlled Merlin *'Mayflower'*, re-gauged for the day but as we ran on 45mm we had no stock we could take to assemble a train. We admired the 32mm stock on view and made all the right noises but regrettably no one felt brave enough to allow either of us to borrow any stock at all and we ran light engine for the afternoon! All the other locos on the day were manually controlled and we felt that the assembled group somewhat disapproved of new fangled radio control. In truth we had felt as welcome as slugs in a lettuce patch!

16mm Association

Despite this previous experience I bravely decided to take up Chris's kind offer to attend the Timpdon Lake open day on a Sunday afternoon in October 2000. I recall the weather was a little on the chilly side but I was soon cheered by the warm welcome from Chris and the other members of the Lancashire and District group.

Word that I ran on 45mm had preceded my visit' but unlike my previous encounter there was a genuine interest in what I was doing. There was even another member who arrived during the afternoon who also ran on 45mm.

The very same Merlin Mayflower, *Emma*, accompanied me on my visit but I still had no 32mm stock. With my past experience I had expected, once again, to have to run light engine but, to my delight, one of the assembled gang freely offered to me the use of his rake of fine looking coaches.

We steamed up and for once *Emma* behaved herself in public. Usually when I try to show her off she decides not to

Above: **Single Fairlie** *Berwyn Belle* **is seen here approaching Accuba bridge with a rake of ancient four wheelers - a bouncy ride I suspect - although the driver looks comfortable enough. The Track is becoming nicely overgrown at this point.**

Right: **Driver Bob checks his watch before preparing to couple up to his train for the return journey. One of the other drivers looks on admiring** *Emma's* **fine lines. The other driver is the Early Learning Centre farmer with added facial hair and a repaint.**
Emma, **a Merlin** *'Mayflower'* **0-4-0, named after our eldest daughter, was the RT's first working live steam loco. She arrived in 1992 and has been altered and improved in the RT workshops over the years. She now has a small coalbunker on the back of the cab, which hides the aerial for the newly fitted 40meg receiver. When new she was fitted with a 27meg set but the upgrade has made a big improvement to her controllability.**

co-operate but on the day she did very well and received deserved praise for her attractive lines. I had after all spent some time the night before giving her a good clean and polish to make sure all the brass bits shone, which afterwards seemed all worth while. After a successful run, somewhat relieved I returned the stock in one piece to its considerate but I suspect also relieved owner.

I stayed and chatted with my new friends until darkness fell and finally left for home content that I had enjoyed a splendid afternoon. It had after all been ten years since my last and rather

Left: Passing trains, *Berwyn Belle* awaits the arrival of *Rachel* at Allington Station on a busy summer weekend service. The coaches are a mix of scratch built stock and converted Bachmann passenger cars. The station building nestles nicely into the greenery.

Lower: Wickham inspired trolley for the track maintenance team. This is a timber bodied scratch built effort which was supposed to be a quickie built on a chassis from a toy truck but developed into a more time consuming project. The chassis proved unreliable and has been replaced with an IP Engineering budget chassis. The driver is, yes you've guessed it, a Tamiya figure.

less enjoyable garden visit. On the Monday morning I posted off my application to rejoin the Association and since that day I have had the great pleasure of visiting and running on most of the lines of the regular members of the group. Occasionally we have even travelled further afield to the wilds of Yorkshire.

Although I was happy as a lone modeller for many years, I would certainly recommend joining the 16mm Association to anyone. One of the main advantages of membership is the chance to visit other modeller's garden lines but, even if this is not for you, the magazine alone is well worth the subscription fee.

On a personal note I have found that my perceived resistance to us 45mm men getting involved to be unfounded. I have met and enjoyed the company of a mixed group of modellers and have been inspired, encouraged and helped whenever I needed 'technical support'.

I will list no names in an attempt to protect the innocent and more importantly not to miss anyone out, but they know who they are - thanks to you all for the help and the friendship.

Equally important to the running of the trains has been the opportunity to socialise with like minded souls and these events also give our partners a chance to compare notes on how the modelling disease has effected their loved ones!

Incredible Depth of Field

Since my early teens I have had an interest in taking photographs. My own line and the others I have been lucky enough to visit, have proved a continual source of photo opportunities. I have been using digital cameras only for the past couple of years and the main advantage for me is the ability to take a full day's shoot home and be able to view them straight away. One of the particular advantages of digital photography for modellers, is

the incredible depth of field, which is a great advantage when taking photos of any model scene.

I have no problem with the concept of 'improving' the 'as taken' shot by painting out any unwanted distractions to whatever degree I feel fit and the trick, as always, is knowing when to stop. The best advice I could pass on to anyone who may be keen on taking photos of their own line is to bend your knees! Buy yourself a kneeling mat from your local garden centre and get right down to track level to take your pictures - you'll be amazed at the results - particularly if you use a tripod or beanbag to ensure sharpness!

Despite having been out in the garden for the past fifteen years, I have had no desire to come back indoors - although I am allowed in for meals and to change for work. I do still dabble with smaller scales and an OO scale GWR branch line lives in the loft, but it is very much a second best to the 16mm garden line. I have mad moments of inspiration, perhaps for a new track alteration or maybe a new item of stock, but then I remember all the half finished projects on the go and the un-built kit in the cupboard. Even so I find it's always the latest project that seems to offer the most promise!

From April to October I look forward to meeting up on the odd weekend with fellow sixteen millers in our local group. I'll also be out and about at the odd exhibition with Chris MacKenzie and his 'Timpdon Sheds' exhibition layout, so why not come up and say hello!

I would like to say a final word of thanks to Sharon, Emma and Rachel for allowing me to invade the garden with my 16mm world!

The Life and Times of the Foxfields Light Railway

Trained as a professional photographer and working on several newspapers during his very successful career, *John Fox* is now happily retired from the newspaper industry and has spent at least some of the last nine years constructing the Foxfields Light Railway in his 30ft x 36ft Manchester garden. Sadly these evocative photographs reflect a railway that is now part of garden railway history as John and Jennifer have recently moved house. The 'train set' is therefore currently packed in boxes, awaiting its re-birth some 300 miles away from where it all began.

John is not only an excellent modeller and something of a model engineer, but has applied his artistic skills to the production of a fully believable garden railway with many striking and original features. The new garden in the South of England measures some 120ft x 18ft and I am very much looking forward to seeing just what will be created in Foxfields Part 2 - 'The Sequel!'

"You've done what in your garden...?" "A harbour you say, with trains". "Yes, that's right and with real water as well". Pause for a few seconds thought. "Won't it flood when it rains?" comes the next bit as their mind ticks over. "Yes, but only if I put the plug in to stop it leaking" I say, and so it goes on.

This conversation has been repeated many times since I set out to build a realistic model harbour scene on the Foxfields Light Railway.

The spark of inspiration for this particular chunk of madness came from an article in an American magazine where the contributor had built an amazing OO gauge harbour-side scene, including a train ferry. If this cameo had been photographed in your 'average' attic with a bit of pale blue paper as a background, it would still have been a brilliant photo, but they decided to take the whole thing and set it up out of doors on the edge of a lake no less. The resulting pictures were absolutely stunning, with the 'plastic' water on the model blending perfectly into the real water and real coastal background. I was hooked!

Now for the hard bit - how do you pick up a large chunk of garden railway and transport it to the coast? Well the answer is you don't, but with the help of an 8ft x 4ft colour

One Sunday afternoon whilst visiting a garden railway layout in Lancashire, I got chatting to another visitor Alex Milne, and soon discovered that he had also been to Majorca and had come home with 'the bug' to build something Majorcan. He chose to make a model of one of the Puerto Soller trams. Once he found out that I had a model of Soller Station newly built in my garden a visit was arranged so that this photo opportunity could be fully explored. The resulting picture speaks for itself.

Above: When Alex Milne turned up to play trains for the day, a scratch-built Puerto Soller tram wasn't the only 'goody' that appeared. Lurking in another box was a wonderful model of a Double Fairlie loco. Once in steam it provided us with some brilliant photo opportunities as it purred round the Foxfields track pulling Alex's scratch-built coaches.

Left: This is where the Majorca connection started. On a visit with Jenny in June 2000 we rode on the Orange Grove Express and I fell in love with everything to do with this railway. Once home, and armed with some two hundred photographs, a couple of guide books and a lot of enthusiasm, I set about recreating Soller Station and some of its rolling stock. It took some twelve months of modelling to recreate the cameo in my garden. Firstly, I made a cardboard corn-flake box model of the station to get to grips with major dimensions such as height, width and length. Then I transferred this to a paper plan, which in turn generated fairly accurate measurements from which the plastic was cut to build the model. I think you will agree that the model does capture the essence of the original station. At the time this photo was taken some small detailing work had yet to be done to finish the model i.e. a clock and the ticket office board. The concrete platform is twelve feet long and was cast in one afternoon's frantic work of cement mixing and laying so that it dried as one long piece. Some three years on and it still hasn't shown any sign of cracking proving one thing, that if you put down good foundations for your model railway, the reward will be lovely smooth running track that will give enjoyment for many years to come. Talking of which, the base and walls that form the foundation for Soller are made from 4ins & 6ins wide, 18ins x 9ins concrete blocks. By 2004 I had used some two hundred and forty blocks in the construction of the FLR - enough for a big house extension.

photo that I had taken of Newhaven Harbour when I visited Sussex, I did manage to bring a harbour scene right into my Manchester garden.

The whole scene sits in a corner by the shed just waiting for me to go and 'play' trains and take pictures. When you look out the back windows the vista is there day and night come rain, sunshine, or snow. I normally leave the plug out so the harbour drains naturally, but if a photo opportunity with the trains and

Above: What more can I say, it's just a 'die for' Roundhouse *'Darjeeling'* loco and it's *sat* on the quayside at Newhaven Harbour on *my* railway. It's not mine of course, but a very welcome visitor on one of last year's open days for the FLR. If you are interested, the low relief building behind the Darj is actually part of the shed door. (The real 12ins to 1ft gauge concrete shed that is). So one must *not* open the door when a train is going past or it gets expensive.

Centre: I first laid eyes on this yellow monster at one of the shows about three or four years ago and immediately fell in love with the fabulous amount of detail on it. It is actually an American Plymouth Switcher made by Accucraft Trains and is part of their 'Classic' Series. I did not see another one at any of the shows until Llanfair in Wales last year. I had already visited the Accucraft stand where I was informed that said switcher had been discontinued. I was gutted. I had lost my chance of owning one of these lovely models so you can imagine my joy as I walked into the next exhibition hall only to find one for sale at the Back 2 Bay Six stand. A quick phone call to my wife Jenny to tell her of my find and I was the proud owner of a wicked yellow diesel. Now some of you will be thinking wait a minute this diesel is 45mm gauge only and runs from track power. Yes, I know that, but the whole loco is bolted together and over the next few months I am going to make it dual gauge and also install ni-cad cells and radio control so it can be used on my railway. I am also going to weather it down a bit as it is bit bright at the moment...

Lower: This is another view of the track work outside Soller Station on the FLR. The coaches are part of a rake of eight IP Engineering kits including one bogie coach. These make a most realistic and satisfying sound as they run through the scratch built point work.

Above: A lovely early summer's afternoon view of Soller Station and sidings with a rake of four Soller coaches in the background and my 'Lady Anne' class *Jennifer* simmering on the platform road. The rake of realistically loaded wagons belongs to Phil Gower, a regular visitor to FLR metals. The wagons are fully sprung and all loads are correctly secured and tied down as per real practice.

Centre: This is my own much-modified Roundhouse 'Lady Anne' locomotive No 10 *Jennifer* named after my long-suffering wife. After its second rebuild, the loco now sports manual forward/reverse radio controlled regulator, a very loud radio controlled steam whistle, a chuff effects unit using live steam, plus working drain cocks. In addition the loco now has a working headlamp and a scale model backhead in the cab, which also has room for three or four model figures - unlike the production version that had a cab full of metal bits and batteries. The chassis and smokebox have been repainted matt black and the gas supply now resides in the left hand side tank. I am currently working on building an even louder chuff unit and finish installing new front and rear headlamps using Roundhouse 'Darj' bits. Apart from the above it's a bog standard *'Lady Anne'* loco... well almost!

Lower: The points are all handmade using redwood or oak sleepers. The lovely carpet of moss grows quite naturally on the track due to its rather damp and shady location. I have filed 'V' grooves into all track joints and when a loco and carriages come rattling through the junction towards Soller Station, the clicketty-clack of the wheels over the joints really has to be heard to be believed. I often spend ten minutes or so at the end of a session pushing the coaches backwards and forwards, by hand, over the multiple point work, just to hear the wonderful sound it makes. Happiness is!

Above: **If you were to buy a commercial version of a railcar like this it could cost hundreds of pounds, yet the whole thing was put together, at very little cost, by Chris Mackenzie with bits from his scrap box. By using an old IP Engineering coach body, a motor and some lorry bits, he managed to build a wonderful railcar for his Timpdon Lake portable layout that frequents the exhibition circuit. It is pictured on the turntable at FLR and we spent a very enjoyable afternoon running it round the garden.**

Right: **Look at this gorgeous vertical-boilered freelance locomotive, which was built from scratch by Dave Wilding in his workshop. It is butane fired and drives two oscillating cylinders running through 4.1:1 reduction gears to a jack shaft, which in turn is coupled to the axle cranks by triangular coupling rods. When fired up and running it has two distinct characteristics. One, it waddles down the track at a very sedate pace, giving off a most satisfying sound of gears whirring, cylinders clanking and chimney chuffing. Two, if you happen to try and run your own loco afterwards then you won't get up any of the hills because Dave's loco is very generous with its oil distribution, mostly onto my track! Yet this powerful loco will pull 70 axles up any hill you can throw at it. The only thing that will make the wheels slip is if it hits a buffer stop. This loco picked up a well-deserved trophy in the 16mm Society 'Modeller of the Year' Competition a couple of years back.**

boats arises, I simply pop the plug in the hole and fill the harbour up with 20-30 gallons of water and add a dash of food colouring to tint it blue to match the photo. After 2-3 hours the water seeps away through the ground because the harbour scene is built on top of a concrete slab pathway leading to the shed. All I have done is to cover the path with very small aquarium grit

Above: **Alex Milne's Roundhouse *'Russell'* glides round the bottom curve with a rake of scratch-built coaches. My *'Lady Anne'* is heaving a ten coach train up the 1 in 36 trestle bridge incline only to be retarded further by hitting a four foot radius curve before coasting back down another 1 in 36 to the bottom curve. This is a real R/C train driver's delight (or nightmare) because unless you concentrate the train will run away and impale itself in a bush or wall. Sounds drastic but much more fun than a boring old level track. I've never been a subscriber to the flat earth society.**

Left: **It looks steep, and it is steep. The 1 in 36 trestle bridge on the Foxfields Light Railway is a real challenge for any locomotive. This section of the track is only used by anyone running a radio controlled or geared locomotive and coaches. The rest turn off and take an easier route round the garden. Martin Boyle's new Roundhouse *'Katie'* gets put through its paces pulling a rake of IP Engineering coaches and scratch-built GVT guards van up the slippery slope and yes, a certain very oily geared loco had got there first. This caused the Katie to spin its wheels as it neared the top of the trestle. This area of the garden has been the subject of many a video shoot, recording the antics of flailing locomotives as they struggle up the 1 in 36 with their heavy loads.**

and let nature do the rest. The whole pathway is now covered with moss and tiny weeds, just like a real harbour would be.

In Grand Isolation

If you are attempting to build any sort of harbour scene outdoors then can I offer the following advice for ageing the quayside timbers. Firstly, use redwood/mahogany for everything wooden. It is then liberally coated with dark oak Cuprinol or similar and when it has soaked in for a couple of hours take a jar full of dry cement and sprinkle it all over the timber. This instantly turns it

a grotty grey colour. Work the cement into the grain using a 1ins paintbrush. When it's done, just walk away and leave it. Nature will do the rest.

The 8ft x 4ft photo itself has been scanned from a 400 ASA 35mm colour negative and professionally printed onto an adhesive plastic which is then stuck onto 6mm plastic backing board and laminated. I'm told it will be okay outdoors for four years before it starts to fade. This was in the year 2000 and technology has moved on, especially with digital cameras, with five to eight megapixel cameras now the norm. Okay, some folk will say that this is cheating and, well yes, I suppose it is, but remember the

Above: **A hot lazy summer's afternoon on the Foxfields Light Railway coaling yard sees a visiting Archangel Fairlie *'Little Wonder'* cooling off after its first run on FLR metals. The loco was supplied new in black, but has been modified by Barry Milner, who installed gas firing and radio control. Alex Milne (who owns the loco) has then completely repainted and lined the loco.**

Centre: **This rake of four Soller scratch built coaches took the best part of two years to finish in between other projects. They started life as eight Bachmann 'Reefer' cars that I cut up and extended to one and a half times their former length. The double side doors were filled in and twelve windows cut on each side. The models have plywood roofs and aluminium angle for the chassis and each coach measures some 2ft long. The wheels and bogies are Bachmann from their coaching stock. One of the major problems of running stock this length on a small garden railway is that eventually you will come to a couple of 3ft reverse curves as you enter sidings etc. Conventional chains and buffer contact is strictly out, as the overhang would give buffer lock and cause a major derailment, so the coaches are coupled together using a vertical pin at one end of the chassis and a pivoting bar at the other end.**

Lower: **The three coaches to the right are IP Engineering four-wheelers built and hand painted by myself. Each coach took about two weeks to paint, as time had to be allowed to dry between coats. The luggage van was completely scratch-built by Dave Wilding, who even CNC milled all the side and end panels of the coach in his workshop. After assembly he asked me if I could do a paint job on it, so I did and it painted up a real treat. It also has a compensated chassis and is dual gauge 32 and 45mm.**

Above: One of the joys of having a garden railway is that when friends turn up to 'play trains' they are likely to bring some pretty exotic and beautiful rolling stock and locos with them as well. In this photo at Newhaven Harbour, we see two of Sam Sparkes' gorgeous engines, made from Mamod and Meccano parts - so they were not expensive. The finish and detailing on these two meths fired locos is amazing and just shows what can be achieved using budget locos and a bit of workshop sweat and skill.

Left: Yet another lovely summer's day on the FLR (who says it always rains in Manchester) and this time my *'Millie' Jenny Wren* is pictured waiting to be filled with water prior to a run. The water tower holds up to two litres and the flow of water is controlled by sliding two brass tubes together until the holes match up. Water then runs down a rubber tube (half of a sausage balloon used at parties to make funny animals) into the loco boiler. The rubber even ripples as the water passes down it, just like the real thing. How sad is that?

clever attic dwellers amongst us train enthusiasts have probably turned several forests full of trees into blue sky paper and pretty backgrounds to wrap around their train layouts over the last 50 years or so. All we are doing is playing catch-up.

The one thing I would definitely recommend is to join up with whatever local branch of the 16mm Association, G-scale Society or Gauge 1 Association (as appropriate) you can find in your area.

I had worked in grand isolation for some seven years before discovering that I wasn't alone on this planet. I have made loads of new friends over the last three years simply by joining the local club and generally have had a marvellous time all round. There is nothing to match a quiet sunny day spent playing trains in the garden with a couple of like minded mates for company, or the thrill of running on someone else's garden railway for the first time. The sheer variety of 'die for' locomotives and rolling stock that have turned up at the Foxfields Light Railway in the last three years is amazing and I would have had to save up for twenty years to get all this kit.

Enough said, I will let the photographs and captions do the rest of the talking!

Steam Locomotives of the AVR-
The Archangel Years

David Pinniger had a good start as a small boy with Hornby clockwork O gauge and then graduated to Hornby Dublo three-rail. Holidays with his family to the Isle of Man and mid-Wales planted the narrow gauge seed. He built many engines and various layouts in 7mm scale 16.5mm gauge but then got hooked on 16mm steam in the garden in 1975. The Ambledown Valley Railway was started in 1981 and this has evolved over the years with his wife Becky providing the garden inspiration. David shares ownership of two 5 inch gauge GWR locos but still gets huge enjoyment from collecting and running 16mm engines.

In the days when my own back garden was still an adventure playground for my two small sons, I enviously devoured the articles written by David Pinniger, Dave Rowlands and Jack Wheldon in various modelling magazines. In fact when I first met David I remember being quite surprised at his comparative youth - I suppose because I was somehow expecting a grizzled old engineer...

When I think back on how I managed to get so hooked on narrow gauge steam in the garden, I realize that Dave Rowlands has a lot to answer for. In the early 1970s, he had built a 32mm gauge line in his garden in Iver and we used to run a mixture of battery powered 16mm narrow gauge and the occasional O-gauge 2 rail train. Dave had then been persuaded to order a 16mm steam engine from Archangel Models after reading Jack Wheldon's evocative articles 'Raising the Pressure' and 'Tracks for the Great Outdoors' in the *Railway Modeller*. I well remember that happy day in 1975 when we collected his long-awaited *'Brick' Lucy* from Stewart Browne at High Wycombe. *'Brick'* was a chunky and rather ugly 0-4-0T with a large single cylinder between the frames. This was a potboiler in the true tradition, the heat being generated by a row of wicks directly under the boiler. But, unlike the earlier products of Bowman and Bassett Lowke, the flames were given plenty of combustion space and were shielded by the side tanks. In addition, the boiler was large enough to give a good head of steam and the meths supply was a simple low-slung tank.

Although both of us were newcomers to live steam, we spent a wonderful afternoon running the new engine which steamed faultlessly round and round Dave's undulating Alderbrook Valley line. At the end of the afternoon, I was another convert to 16mm steam as I realized that at last here was the 'real thing' and I went home to work out if I could raise enough cash to buy an Archangel engine. I eventually sold my collection of 0-gauge Hornby tinplate and ordered a 'Princess' from Stewart Browne. But more about that engine later.

The performance of the first *'Brick'* became legendary. The trial of the prototype model on the Jack Wheldon's Border Counties was conducted in a gale, which blew the train off the track but *'Brick'* kept on going. Jack's account in the *Railway Modeller* of this elevation of the humble pot boiler from a glorified toy to a practical working engine inspired many others to follow. Dave's *'Brick' Lucy* gave many years trusty service on his Alderbrook Valley Railway but, when this line sadly decayed and went the way of the original Welsh Highland, Dave lent AVR No 1 to my father. He then ran it on many garden railways, including my own Ambledown Valley in Cookham, and it was eventually transferred here permanently. *Lucy* is now a mature lady some thirty years of age and only appears on the line a few times a year. She is much loved and still steams well but has an increasingly loud knock from her big end. She also has a tendency to self-reverse her slip eccentrics on the bank if given a heavy train.

AVR No 7 *Lord Snowdon*, an Archangel single Fairlie 0-6-4T, pauses at Holman's Cottage with a mixed goods on the Ambledown Valley Railway. The engine is a meths-fired potboiler with two outside cylinders.

Above: **Period piece in Bishops Amble yard. AVR No 4 *Lousia* is on the steaming bay, No 1 *Lucy* is on the left and AVR No 6 *Thomas The Rhymer* is in the background.**

Left: **'Caledonia' constructed from a Lindale kit in 1979 has its first steaming on the AVR before being painted. Not long after this, the wheels fell off and had to be replaced.**

Copper 'Porcupine Quills'

The proceeds from the sale of my Hornby tinplate provided just enough capital to acquire my first Archangel steam engine, which was AVR No 2 *Princess Hester*. This used the *'Brick'* boiler and chassis but in a rather more aesthetically pleasing engine which was a massively overscale version of the original Festiniog *'Prince'* 0-4-0T. *Princess Hester*, with its increased weight and better heat shielding, turned in performances on the AVR that even eclipsed the *'Brick'*. The engine ran miles on the Alderbrook Valley railway and then for some years on my Ambledown Valley Railway. It ran for a few years with a home-built cab and tender but strangely, was rarely photographed in this condition. *Princess Hester* then started to suffer from wear in the eccentrics and main crank, which made it self-reverse even on a light train. Jack Wheldon's *'Brick'* had also worn out and Jack's solution was to rebuild the engine with two cylinders with the valves operated by his Wheldon/Tayleur gear. The result was *'Superbrick'*, not an engine of great beauty, but one that would pull every single vehicle that we could hang on the back. Jack kindly offered to rebuild my *'Princess'* in the same way but I was a little reluctant to trust Jack with the aesthetics of the bodywork. We eventually

Right: The engine that started it all, Alderbrook Valley No 1 *Lucy*. The engine is an Archangel meths-fired single cylinder 'Brick' 0-4-0T. Here she is in 1985 running as Ambledown Valley Railway No 1. The engine is virtually as purchased in 1975 with the addition of a brass dome and nylon buffers.

Centre: As yet unpainted, *Princess Hester* is on trial on Jack Wheldon's Border Counties Railway. She is steaming through Mutely Standing on a test train.

Lower: Now resplendent in maroon paint, *Princess Hester* explores the further reaches of the Border Counties Railway.

agreed that Jack would build the chassis and boiler and hand the working engine to me to finish off the body. Jack used the original potboiler but added three rows of copper 'porcupine quills' to improve heat transfer. He also made a new cylinder and moved and modified the original Archangel one to the outside. The old 0-4-0 now became an outside-framed 2-6-0T with four original Archangel driving wheels and two more turned from Stewart's castings. Jack also made a slightly different version of his outside valve gear that is rather on the heavy side and more marine than railway in appearance. However, it ran well and so I set about building a suitable body based on a shortened version of an Irish narrow gauge engine. Jack wrote about the rebuild in an article in *Practical Model Railways* entitled 'Princess Hester's Transformation' which was the last article he ever wrote as, very sadly, he died suddenly in 1988 before it appeared in print in March 1989. *Princess Hester* is looking very scruffy these days and really needs a repaint but she is still very powerful and runs very well and the safety valve is as flatulent as ever.

My next engine was yet another Archangel, but this time it was a one-off 0-6-0ST called *Louisa* based loosely on a quarry Hunslet. I fell in love with this engine when I first saw it in Stewart Browne's shed at High Wycombe but I was told that it did not steam well because of insufficient air getting to the fire. I suggested a very non-technical solution of drilling some holes in the saddle tank. A short time later Stewart rang me to say that he had done the butchery and it had indeed solved the problem. In 1976 *Louisa* became AVR No 4 and she soon proved to be a very different engine from the others. This was because she had a single inside cylinder, which at ⅜ins bore, was much smaller than the ⁹⁄₁₆ins of the 'Brick'. Although powerful when going, she was trickier to start and had a tendency to accelerate like a grey-hound to reach a very unprototypical speed of 150mph. I eventually built a tender to house a radio control battery and receiver and put a servo on the regulator. This made the engine much more

Above: **Early days on Dave Rowland's Alderbrook Valley Railway. AVR No 4** *Louisa,* **a meths-fired single cylinder potboiler waits with Sedimentary Sand and Gravel Company works train. Passing on the main line is AVR No 3** *Hazel,* **an internally-fired Archangel** *Rheidol* **2-4-0T.**

Lower: **AVR No 1** *Lucy* **at Bishops Amble having done 30 years of running without an overhaul.**

manageable but eventually she suffered from the common Archangel disease of worn eccentrics. Rather than rebuild her, *Louisa* was sold in 1989 to the Olsons in the USA and, as far as I know, she is still there.

The Archangel engine I had always lusted after was the powerful two-cylinder *'Snowdon Ranger'.* This engine was based on the North Wales Narrow Gauge 0-6-4T and like the prototype, was a true single Fairlie with a swinging front power bogie. These engines soon acquired an enthusiastic following as they were very docile and had a wonderful rolling gait on the uneven 16mm track often encountered in those early days. I remember the price - £299 - a large sum of money all those years ago and well beyond my modest means.

Characteristic Archangel Flatulence

I still hankered after a *'Snowdon Ranger'* and in 1977 I was very lucky to be offered a second-hand one, which was only two years old and this became AVR No 7 *Lord Snowdon.* With two big cylinders and a big potboiler this engine would pull everything we had on the Alderbrook Valley Railway. The engine also ran slowly and sedately and, unlike our single cylinder engines, self-started on banks with no hesitation. The articulation was attractive to watch but led to some problems when trying to start the engine from cold. Condensed water in the big cylinders would cause the wheels to lock and the normal method of pushing down on the engine to force the water through did not work. The engine had another annoying habit of setting fire to the scenery. This was because there was a long meths filler pipe that went from the meths tank amidships to the front buffer-beam. This would ignite so that the engine was a mobile flaming

Right: **AVR No 4 *Louisa*, now running on the Ambledown Valley Railway with a cab and tender constructed in Cookham Works. She is also fitted with single channel radio on the regulator to try and calm her 'runaway train' tendencies.**

Lower: **Something of a historical photograph from the camera of Peter Dobson. *Thomas the Rhymer* approaches Amble Junction with the afternoon passenger train to Woody End.**
Peter Dobson

torch, which set light to overhanging plants. I eventually cut the long meths filler pipe and made a new short one facing the back of the engine.

'*Snowdon Ranger*' was in standard black when I bought it but I repainted first in NWNGR dark red. When that burnt and blistered in the heat from the meths wicks, I tried sage green car engine enamel and this coat of paint lasted 25 years, from 1978 to 2003. For many years *Lord Snowdon* was the main engine of the AVR and was the first engine to run on my own Ambledown Valley Railway in Cookham in 1980. By the early nineties *Lord Snowdon* was getting very scruffy and unloved and it was sold to raise money for another engine.

A few years passed and I rediscovered the attraction of the simple potboiler and regretted selling *Lord Snowdon*. Luckily, the friend who had bought the engine said that if I really wanted it back, I could have it. The engine was dismantled and the body parts went in the post for stove enamelling. The body parts came back beautifully finished in red: at last, *Lord Snowdon* would have the intended NWNG livery. The first run was on a cold windy day. Would the engine run after all this time? *Lord Snowdon* went round like a trooper, safety valve blowing off with the characteristic Archangel flatulence. Although *Lord Snowdon* is maybe not quite as smooth on the self-starting as it was in 1977, the engine runs remarkably well for its age and provenance. Although cosmetically restored, it has had no mechanical attention at all and is a testament to the durability of Archangel models. I am looking forward to many more years of happy running with *Lord Snowdon*.

The original owner of the '*Snowdon*' also sold me his Archangel '*Rheidol*' 2-4-0 sidetank built in 1976. This engine which became AVR No 6 *Thomas The Rhymer* was based on the 2ft gauge Bagnall built for the Plynlimon and Hafan

tramway and then transferred to the Vale of Rheidol Railway. This was very different from our potboilers as it had a meths-fired Smithies boiler and a single inside cylinder, the outside cylinders being dummies. Dave Rowlands had an identical engine also built in 1977 called '*Hazel*'. These were powerful engines with a $\frac{9}{16}$ins bore cylinder and much more docile than the early versions with a small $\frac{3}{8}$ins diameter bore cylinder. Although the '*Rheidols*' were [and still are] fun to operate, they had a very small water capacity in the boiler which meant that they had to be continually watched and water pumped in from the side tanks at regular intervals. After a few years, I cut down the high bunker meths tank so that it was level with the side tanks and built a full cab. The engine was sold a few years ago to operate on the planned Garth End Railway in Yorkshire. But sadly, the railway has not

Above: Lord Snowdon **resplendent in red after a repaint at Bishops Amble in 2004.**

Left: **Archangel** *'Prince of Wales'* **in service on the AVR and hauling an appropriate train.**

yet been built and the only time the engine has run in recent years is when it revisited its old haunt at Bishops Amble.

Vintage Running Days

The next engine was completely different from the Archangels, being built from a kit made by a long defunct company called Lindale. It was loosely based on the Isle of Man Railway 0-6-0T *'Caledonia'*. As the prototype loco is 3ft gauge this was a big engine on 32mm gauge. In 1979 this engine was a real pioneer as it was for simple screwdriver assembly with all the machining

and soldering done. It was also attractively packaged and Jack Wheldon wrote a comprehensive review in the August 1981 issue of *Model Railways*. I had great fun putting this engine together and, as I am no model engineer, it really was a test of the quality of the design that everything fitted. When the body was finished I added *Foxdale* nameplates and the engine became AVR No 8. The great day came when I packed the asbestos wicks, filled the tank with meths and lit the fire. After what seemed an interminable time, the pressure gauge crept up to 40 psi and I opened the regulator in the cab. Nothing happened! The engine refused to move. Then I remembered the choke regulator in the smokebox - which was shut hard. When I opened this, there was a loud gurgle, a gout of hot steam and oil from the chimney and *Foxdale* moved for the first time under her own steam. What a feeling of elation that this box of bits had been transformed into a working engine! Many other modellers since have written of experiencing a similar feeling after successfully putting a Roundhouse kit together.

Foxdale did need a lot of running in and there were a few teething troubles. The worst was when the driving wheels fell off the axles! An improved replacement set of wheels from Lindale cured this but then the coupling and connecting rods

Right: AVR No 8 *Foxdale* visits the Border Counties Railway in 1980. The engine is now painted red with new wheels and other additions, including a new brass dome and cab steps to hide the meths tank.

Centre: Another 'blast from the past'! AVR No 4 *Louisa* is loaned from the Ambledown Valley to the Sedimentary Sand & Gravel Company for the workmen's train (one 'pneumonia' coach and a coal truck). The AVR office is in the background.

Lower: AVR No 6 *Thomas The Rhymer* revisiting the AVR after being sold to the Garth End Railway.

disintegrated. We discovered that this was because they were alloy castings and the heat from the fire had weakened them to the point of failure. Under Jack's guidance, I made up some new ones from nickel silver and these are still OK twenty-five years on. Once the problems were sorted out, the engine was very powerful and the exhaust choke regulator meant that she would run very slowly on a load up the banks. No 8 ran miles on my AVR and other lines but then started to lose compression and power. Colin Edwards had a similar problem with his *'Caledonia'* and diagnosed worn cylinder rings. It was a simple matter to renew these and restore the engine's performance to as good as new. She is still a good runner and comes out on the line on our 'Vintage Running Days'.

The last engine in the AVR Archangel series, a Vale of Rheidol *'Prince of Wales'* 2-6-2T, was actually acquired much later. This engine with two cylinders, slip eccentric gear and internal meths firing, was for many years the flagship of the Archangel works. The first ones were built in 1973 and, with various modifications, they were made for over fifteen years. Originally built with a Smithies boiler, like the *'Rheidol'* mentioned earlier, Stewart Browne designed a very efficient fire tube boiler for the later ones. My loco was originally built in 1982 for Bill Abbott, who was one of the founders of the 16mm Association, and it was his pride and joy. When he sadly died in 1999, I bought the engine, together with three matching Archangel bogie coaches. *'Prince of Wales'* is one of my favourite engines, the balance between steam generation and cylinders is exactly right and so it is a beautiful runner. Even though it is over twenty years old and for detail cannot compare with more modern versions, it is still much admired and is a great example of a really good bit of 16mm model engineering.

Thirty years after I first got the steam bug, I am still well and truly hooked. I have got far too many engines for such a small line but can never resist the lure of yet another prototype or an example from a different 16mm loco builder.

A Tale of Two Mamods

Born in 1960 when families still took off to the West Country for summer seaside holidays behind diesel hydraulics and steam trains, *Dudley Hubbard* has been interested in all things railway since childhood when his parents tried in vain to pull him off a kids train ride at Sandown on the Isle of Wight.

Describing himself as a modeller, the approach to garden railways that he favours is one of individual atmosphere and ambience; one where the stock and railway has a unique feel about it and which includes input from the owner. More in fact, than just running trains straight out of the box. He's not so keen on the highly polished narrow gauge locomotives - even more so if there's no crew in the cab. He took up voluntary editorship of SMT; the magazine of the Association of 16mm Narrow Gauge Modellers for three years from issues 88 - 100 when he finally cracked and passed the baby over to someone else. One aspect of trains that he definitely doesn't like is rushing for them in the morning when he makes his way to work. For the past twenty years this has been as a photographer in a popular London museum. He currently lives in Surrey.

Steam-oil, water and meths, gas or coal make our steam locos run. As they warm-up, water drips from a pipe and as the needle nudges ever-upwards very small whiffs of steam appear. The safety valve lifts and a huge plume of smoke shoots up to the sky. There's a sizzle from somewhere and you can smell the hot beastie just waiting to be driven with soft nimble fingers. The loco gets extremely hot and splutters oil and water at you just as you lean over to check the pressure. This is REAL railway with hefty steel wheels, brass bearings and wooden wagon bodies. Three-link chain joins wagon to wagon and they clank and clatter as you start or stop the loco. Pick the stock up and it feels heavy and solid. The track sits outside in all weathers - some rust here and a small amount of moss there. A point freezes solid in the winter and a track panel buckles with the heat of the summer. A gloss painted building fades to matt and starts peeling having been outside for one year.

I work to 16mm/ft narrow gauge running on 32mm gauge track, or 1:19th scale, out in the garden - a project that has been ongoing since 1994. During this time my stock has grown and with it, I hope, some sense of style to make its appearance unique and individual. At full size this would be a two-foot gauge tramway and given that narrow gauge railways come in all shapes and sizes I will say that I prefer rundown, industrial and rustic types. I was looking for a name to sum up this railway and because the road where I live is called Sylvan (of forests, trees) and I'm up on top of a hill (Heights) a friend suggested the *Sylvan Heights (industrial) Tramway*; and that is why you won't see my wagons with the abbreviated name of the railway on the sides!

One aspect that I really enjoy about this particular scale is the complete freedom that we have. Some of the smaller scale railway modellers place more emphasis on history and provenance resulting in more of a bearing on what's run with

what. They often employ the finest of detail. I like to think that our hobby feels less serious, and, dare I suggest, more FUN. I also like the fact that many of our models are made from 'found items' - that is bits of wood, metal or plastic. 16mm grew up as a scratch-builder's scale in the early days and whilst the trade support that we now enjoy is fabulous there is still a large number of us who look at everyday things and exclaim that it could be made into a 16mm so-and-so with a bit stuck on here and that bit chopped off. Do be warned though that this should not be seen as an open invitation to collect clutter! I write from experience...

Easy to Do

It really is the Great Outdoors when you're faced with a wee plot of land, some track and a desire to see something running. Many of my railway circle peers mentioned this; get something up and running as soon as possible. Good advice. Even a little whiff of steam negotiating a small circle can be such a driving force to get on with the job and construct the railway proper. Even better advice is to join your local 16mm group and go run on, and observe, other peoples garden railways.

Like most fellow garden railway enthusiasts I enjoy running 'live steam'. Whilst today we enjoy all manner of these locos with the highest precision, I have to say that there is still a big place in my heart for the humble oscillator, typified by the Mamod and of course the marvellous *'Jane'* from IP Engineering. The two Mamods that I run were my first real steam locos representing good, cheap, entry level locos ten years ago. They were both second-hand and not in the best of condition. This suited me fine because I wanted to turn them into individual locos using some basic modelling skills. They both evolved through observation of favourite pro-

Right: **At the end of every year Robin and Janet Willis open their Surrey garden for us 16mm enthusiasts to steam-in the New Year on their very large circuit. Lots of tea and cakes are consumed and we spend the evening in the garden until well past midnight. Again, lifetime friendships are forged amongst garden railway modellers.**

Left: **An old coarse scale wagon sits in what I'd hoped would become a branch line, but in fact has become a long siding. After eight to ten years outside the track and Rowland's mix has weathered down acceptably.** *Hebe Carl Teschner* **is planted just behind and to the left, while** *Cotoneaster* **is to the right with another variety of the same plant in the left foreground.**

totypes and the small details to be found thereon. The first loco was inspired by the Darjeeling 'B' class locos, which I'd observed at close quarters during a 1982 'walkabout' in India and Pakistan. Their lack of cab backplate made for a larger cab and in model form would make it easier to get operating fingers onto the controls. This seemed like a good approach and meant that I could remove the seemingly narrow doorway from the model. My second Mamod conversion also utilised this cab modification but had arrived on my workbench with a spark arrester chimney which I felt to be more Sittingbourne & Kemsley; so this one had centre buffers, deeper buffer beams - down to rail height - and 'eyelids' over the cab front windows - I copied this last detail from a First World War Baldwin 2-6-0 seen at Amberley museum.

Julian Smith's *Milton No1* **takes a train of tubs up the bank in Suffolk. She is a meths fired Mamod oscillator with modifications such as a silver soldered boiler for a higher working pressure. The presence of the driver gives a centre point to the photo. Try to pre-plan some of your garden railway photography and don't always go for the three quarter front shot. Either take photos OR run a train but don't try both.**

Now I definitely wouldn't describe myself as an engineer or a metalworker and so I limited myself to modifications that were easy to do. Thus with the cab back removed I unscrewed the rear buffers and cut a square section of knot-free Cedar and drilled two holes to match up with the empty buffer holes. 6ba

Left: 'Ogwen' was built from an early/original Maxwell Hemmens kit; but not by me I might add. This gas-fired locomotive was modified several years ago by my friend Jim Mander, because I didn't like the big gas tank stuck inside the cab roof and partly obscuring the cab front windows. Jim took this tank to the back of the cab via a new floor extension, turning the tank through 90 degrees from horizontal to vertical. Her front axle is sprung and has been the cause of endless derailments on my track at home whereas the Mamod locos have no such trouble. Why do manufacturers bother springing 16mm locos when there isn't the mass to keep the loco down? 'Ogwen' was weathered panel by panel; matt black Humbrol enamel was applied to a very small area and almost immediately wiped off with a piece of bathroom tissue.

Centre: Fayles wagons originally from Saltford Models by Brian Clarke. These are some of my first and favourite wagons, having whitemetal wheels and axleboxes, which trundle along really prototypically. One end of each wagon has a headless panel pin protruding down from the buffer beam; at the other end of the wagon a complete panel pin retains a 40 x 6 x 0.5mm brass bar via a small hole. The wagons are linked together by lifting the end with the headless pin and locating this in another hole in the free end of the corresponding bar. Ply body, Plasticard strapping with panel pins carefully applied. Wood treated with Creosote after construction then sprayed with water and dipped into a bag of cement powder!

Lower: Battery power is also highly favoured on the SHT. This little *Tracteur* has a body built from a carefully sliced corned beef tin with a running board from (double glazing) angled aluminium. The chassis is one of those £20 jobs with a motor driving one axle; though is this instance I've superglued twelve-tooth Delrin sprockets to the outside of the wheels on one side of the loco, and linked them with Delrin chain. The silencer behind the driver is a metal film cassette and is linked to a centre-off toggle switch.

nuts and bolts secured this in place. The cab roof was removed and a slightly longer one made from thin brass. This was gradually rolled to match the cab top by getting two old bits of carpet and using a wooden rolling pin carefully to roll from side to side. Because the carpet 'gives' it allows the roof to bend a little. Try it bit by bit and check the roof to the cab at regular intervals. Small countersunk bolts had their flat heads filed down to bare brass, were tinned with solder and positioned into the holes along the cabside top using small nuts to secure them.

Above: Oscillating meths fired superpower seen backing on to a train of heavy (TME) Vale of Rheidol coaches in Suffolk. The three locos started off with five bogie coaches and one four wheeled brake - representing twenty-two axles. After a while one loco dropped out and the other two continued to haul the train, which was eventually increased to thirty-eight axles!

Right: A rampant houseleek *Sempervivum tectorum* is checked out by a member of the SHT staff. *Cotoneaster* grows in the left foreground whilst Alpine strawberries take off in the background to the right.

Lower: Trains? What trains? The height of the summertime on the SHT. *Hebe Carl Teschner* and the tall flowers of *Sempervivum tectorum* in full flower. *Sempervivum arachnoideum* - cobweb houseleeks - and *Golden Pearlwort* help cover the ground. Most of this growth can easily be chopped back prior to running without spoiling the glorious blaze of colour.

In a Rough 'n' Ready Style

Having estimated where the roof sat, allowing for overhang and the correct 'look', I tinned the roof underside with solder in the places where the screw heads touched. With the roof on the cab, it was all checked visually and when happy with the result I ran

Left: **'Britomart'** is an early single cylinder internally meths fired quarry Hunslet from TME. She is seen here in the company of an IP Engineering coach. Note the mossy track, which was made by adding potato water to the Rowland's mix. The thick brown mound on the left is unwanted moss from a neighbour's lawn - which was lifted in chunks and laid straight on top of the concrete foundation at this point of the railway.

a small flame over the roof to melt the solder and join the roof to the fixing screws. In fact one screw either side is all it needs. By drilling into the top outside corners of the wooden cab floor extension - detached from the loco - using a pillar drill, I was able to insert two brass rods for cab back uprights/roof supports. These need only touch the roof underside. A horizontal brace comes from a flat piece of brass midway up the rods and is held in place with a spot of solder. Take your time. A figure placed in the cab gives a good visual check for the correct look. *If it looks right it is right.*

The front end also had the buffers unscrewed and a new deeper bufferbeam - as per many industrial steam locos - was made from standard ¼ins ply and fitted using the existing screw holes on the Mamod. Both front and back buffer beams had big new square dumb buffers made from that Cedar. The visible parts of the boiler, side tanks, cab and roof were rubbed down with emery cloth, the wheels and motion masked with tape and the whole lot sprayed with heat resistant matt black motorcycle exhaust paint. When this was dry and had cured, the side tanks were painted with standard Humbrol matt green.

A white chinagraph pencil enabled a name and number to be written on the tank/cab sides in a rough'n'ready style - well suited to this kind of prototype. Wooden bufferbeams were painted Humbrol matt red. The whole loco was given a wash or two of paint-dirtied white spirit to tone the finish down. A single driver-cum-fireman came from the Tamiya pit-stop crew. Stood correctly on the wooden footplate he had a small drill through his foot into the wood. A piece of fine wire was stuck in his foot, protruding down. This makes for a removable figure, or one that can be turned to the direction of travel. Our narrow gauge loco is now longer with a greater swing on the curves - most prototypical - and you have a unique loco.

Some of these Mamod oscillators are not known for tame running by newcomers but there are a couple of modifications that will make a huge difference. Do bear in mind that when I got my Mamods the IP Engineering *'Jane'* wasn't on the market and *she* tends to come ready fitted with most add-ons that I'm about to describe. After ten years of running, my two meths fired locos have had most modifications known to man. An exhaust regulator made the biggest difference; holding back or throttling the spent steam stops the thing from running off, out of control. My exhaust regulator, made by a friend, sits just behind the smokebox door. It's in the form of an adjustable valve and altering the position of the darts on the smokebox door either opens or closes the valve. An in-line lubricator makes some difference; the steam becomes saturated with *steam oil* before it passes into the cylinders and keeps the thing running sweetly. These lubricators are commercially available at a reasonable cost. A silver soldered boiler got rid of the problem of blowing sight glasses and allowed the steam to work at a greater pressure than before.

I find that the locos will trundle around the sharp curves of my line with great ease and the power they produce is quite amazing, try holding one back! I like the fact that if they stop due to lack of steam they will move off under their own power when the pressure has built up again. I enjoy seeing plenty of steam coming out of the chimney, which they also do well. Being meths fired means they run in the coldest of weather and at all times can be refuelled mid-run.

I hope that this treatise on my little railway helps to inspire others. It doesn't matter *what* you do; just do *something*. For me 16mm is many more things than just railways in the garden. The friends that I've made and whose company I continue to enjoy, the places we've been together, a renewed interest in gardening, local wildlife and even more of a passion for photography.

Above: My *Ogwen* is seen here on the steep climb through
Fredley station on Frank Warren's line, whilst David Kiernan's
Jane romps along in the level cutting. The coach immediately
behind the loco is one of a rake of three that I scratch-built.
Plasticard bodies with a roof made from guttering and riding on
wooden frames with steel wheels. The flat wagon is from the
basic LGB range whilst the hoppers are from MDC Roundhouse
- all with 32mm steel wheelsets on longer axles.

Left: My first Mamod, *Sylvania*, or number 20. Note the dumb
buffers, open cab and matt paint finish as detailed in my write-up.
The cab step just visible below the driver is a whitemetal casting
which has been stuck to the plain end of a bigger transverse
meths tank. The figure stands up by virtue of a metal pin through
his foot into the block of cedar between the dumb buffer and
metal cab floor. As noted the Jim Mander smokebox darts serve
as the exhaust regulator. Now eleven years old, this loco could do
with a repaint.

Right: Underneath the *Box* and *Pittosporum* trees at the far end
of the circuit sits this old 'Big-Big' body, which has been given a
liberal coating of instant rust. 'Mind-your-own-business' blankets
the foreground whilst all sorts of plant oddments tumble off of
the rocks in the background covering the long siding as they go.

The Snitterby & Waddingham Railway

Geoff Thompson grew up in Northumberland within earshot of the East Coast Main Line, with A4 Pacifics rattling the house windows. At school in Ashington, he was never far from the sound of a J27 or Q6 rattling a 1,500ton train of 21ton coal hoppers. In those days, the miners and their families had their own passenger trains, using old NER stock hauled by NCB Austerity tanks.

After qualifying as an Incorporated Engineer, *Geoff* worked in television production and studied education at post-graduate level. Now working in Lincoln University, he lives on the edge of the Lincolnshire Wolds in an early eighteenth century cottage.

Geoff is the garden railway correspondent for *Railway Modeller* magazine and says that, despite being an LNER man through and through, the three standard gauge locomotives he has driven were all GWR. He considers this to be a conspiracy and, as a GWR man myself - I can assure him that this assumption is correct!

When I am at work I am surrounded by state of the art technology; I manage a Media Production Centre with TV and radio studios filled with millions of pounds worth of digital kit. It comes as a surprise to some people when they discover that my greatest passion is railways in the days of steam.

Although I had a train set as a kid of nine or ten (a Triang *Princess Elisabeth* with blood and custard mark one coaches) I

Left: A visiting *'Vale of Rheidol'* locomotive is seen here crossing the viaduct. The double track viaduct is the SWR's most spectacular structure. Eight arches, eight feet long and over one foot high. It is actually marine plywood, the 'sandstone blocks' being oblongs of vinyl floor covering glued in place. It is very sturdily built and, because the piers don't actually touch the ground, it is only supported at each end. Lots of light coloured matt paints provide the base colour, and the predominant sandstone has a smattering of grey and dark green. I think it looks quite convincing.

Right: A visiting Roundhouse *'Vale of Rheidol'* locomotive takes advantage of the only straight piece of track on the SWR. It is true that cold days are best for steam effects, but this loco produces a good show of steam even on this warm summer's day…

did not start railway modelling until the tender age of fifty. Some months before we moved into our present house, I saw a G-scale train set in a shop window. I'd never seen this scale before and was fascinated. My friend Karl was with me at the time, and the subsequent conversation got around to 16mm narrow gauge modelling. I knew Karl built big locomotives for ride-on garden railways, but I didn't know he was a member of the 16mm NGM Association. I joined the society and began subscribing to *GardenRail*.

Once I discovered that 16mm live steam was affordable, I set my heart on a garden railway. When we moved house, the opportunity was there. The south facing garden isn't large by any means, but it doesn't need to be. Luckily it is terraced, providing two terraces separated by a narrow flowerbed, the width of the house and each about 4 metres deep, enough space for table and chairs. Below that was an area about 7.5 metres square, purporting to be lawn, but in reality moss and thistle infested weeds. Clearly, this needed to be made nice to look at.

Cotswold Stone and a Small Pond

What better than a rockery in one corner, raised flowerbeds around the perimeter with dwarf retaining walls of Cotswold stone and a small pond? The fact that a railway could unobtrusively snake through the rockery and flowerbeds was quite secondary, honest! I have to thank Karl for his assistance in gaining the necessary planning permission; Judith had faith in his landscaping abilities, while I had not hitherto shown much gardening potential beyond mowing the lawn occasionally!

The area available for the railway is obviously quite small, and this is where 16mm narrow gauge comes into its own. Narrow gauge railways have tight curves and are modest in scale too. Trains are short, with small locos and stock travelling at slow speeds, often not getting much above 15mph. Stations are often modest affairs with little platforms, and major civil engineering works are usually avoided. The through line of the SWR is only about twice the length of a main line passenger train of the same scale, but it is quite convincing as a narrow gauge railway, providing plenty of interest and a reasonable journey time. 15mph in 16mm scale is only a little over 23 yards per minute.

There are many ways to build a garden railway, and I am not going to suggest that the way we did it was the best, but it works

Left: Matthew (Roundhouse *'Katie'*) by the water tower, with *Marquis* (Cheddar *'Samson'*) passing on the track to the sidings in the shed. Behind are mineral wagons from Hartland, very inexpensive kits, which can be assembled in minutes. The matt grey is cheap automotive aerosol spray; the gloss black is from the 'odds and ends' range. Bachmann style couplings have been replaced with the centre buffer type from Brandbright, designed to fit as a direct replacement. The lettering is Decadry™ lettering purchased from a stationers.

Centre: Battery powered locos are useful for hauling stock out of and into storage, and although most of mine are diesel outline, I do like this battery powered tram. It was made from an IP Engineering kit, and has radio control. Running on 4 AA batteries, it will run for a long time, and has a surprising amount of hauling power.

Lower: The diesel (a battery powered freelance model) was a joint effort by my friend Karl and myself. He built the chassis and I built the body from aluminium sheet and plastic card. It is powered by 8 AA cells and has remote control. It weighs as much as a live steamer, and will haul every item of stock that I own - around thirty-five feet of wagons and coaches. Water cranes look good on the platforms. These examples were from Garden Railway Specialists. They are painted in the SWR's standard drab green.

and has caused few problems so far. We began with a garden shed on the left of the bottom patio, with its narrow side on the edge of the lawn, about 9 inches or 200mm above it. The floor of the shed would house 4 sidings, running lengthways at the rear, with two lines running out through a trapdoor, one to join the main line south and the other west into the station junction. The floor thus provided the all-important datum for the railway. The construction method was quite simple. Single concrete builders blocks were laid along the course of the track, on their edge and lengthways, about one block length apart. Each has a concrete foundation of around 4 to 6 inches (100mm to 150mm) deep, about 50% larger than the base of the blocks. The foundations were, as far as possible, at the datum height, with a peg in each marked with a long spirit level.

Well-treated 12mm marine ply was cut to the trackwork shape, 6ins to 7ins wide for single track, 14ins (350mm) for double and large enough for the whole station area. It was then screwed onto the blocks. The ply was edged with 1ins wide strips of 4mm

Right: The Roundhouse and Cheddar live steamers look well together in SWR livery, seen here in Waddingham station. The Station Master's house is pottery, bought at a show.

Centre: Marquis has a good head of steam charging through Waddingham. The station seemed quite large until the track was down and the trains arrived. It is surprising how much space even a little a country station can occupy.

Lower: This Roundhouse model is incredibly well detailed. The driver bears more than a passing resemblance to a renowned model locomotive designer! Line side huts, platform shelters and factory buildings are cast concrete items from Tuxcraft. These are not highly detailed, but at normal viewing distance they are quite acceptable. They are certainly robust enough to stay outside all year round.

ply, both to give strength and to retain ballast. Narrow foundations were dug for the retaining walls according to the size of rocker or flowerbed, and once the walls were up, the beds filled with rock or soil as appropriate. Because the 'lawn' was beyond redemption, it was sprayed a couple of times with path clearer, and once the vegetation was dead, the sod dug up to help fill the beds before fresh topsoil was added. Although the railway looks as though it runs on these flowerbed 'embankments', the soil does not quite reach the plywood base, allowing a little air to circulate below.

Does Not Dominate

The lawn area slopes to down to the right, so the track is closer to 18ins (0.5m) above it there. In order to give access to the lawn, Karl suggested he would make a lift-out bridge. This magnificent structure, a 1.5m long Ross truss, looked so good that another bridge was discussed, and in due course a 2m long girder bridge spanned the dry riverbed which led away left from the lake (pond). The final civil engineering feat, spanning the dried riverbed to the right of the lake, is a sweeping eight arch double track viaduct, 150 feet in length and 20 feet high (scale!) which links the raised corner flower beds at the bottom of the garden. Although it is made of marine ply, with vinyl 'stones' glued in place, it is very convincing.

So much for the railway being unobtrusive, but although it has some obvious features, it does not dominate the garden. You could lift it out and put topsoil in its place and you'd never know it had been there. Planting has been very much Judith's domain, but near the railway in places where there is a good view of passing trains, sedums and miniature pines provide scale trees and bushes. Every morning I look out from the kitchen and marvel at the railway, and I am pleased to say Judith confessed that she likes to see the railway too. Each development was thoroughly discussed with the domestic authorities for approval, but it is nice to know it is enjoyed rather than just tolerated!

My railway isn't highly detailed by any means. I'm not a very skilled modeller, but I don't think you need to be. Garden

Left: Matthew has been lined out using Trimline™ tape. This self adhesive tape is easy to apply. The ends are trimmed with a modelling knife, and held with a small spot of varnish. The tape is easy to remove, so any errors are easy to remedy. The Roundhouse 'Katie' is quite a chunky model, and I've used the second smallest size of tape. My loco nameplates are from Guilplates, who offer a range of styles and will produce plates or signs to order.

Centre: The truss bridge is made from aluminium, and is designed to lift out to give access to the lawn. When Karl designed and built it, he was inspired to suggest two more bridges and a viaduct!

Lower: The hoppers are Hartland kits, sprayed with grey primer and given the Rustbase rust treatment. The guards van is from R2R Models, one of only two items of SWR stock that I did not make. Although the track appears to run on the flowerbed, the soil does not quite reach the marine plywood track base, which is supported every ½ metre (18ins) on builder's blocks.

railways are not normally viewed close up, so very fine detail is less important to me. Buildings and railway infrastructure stay outside all year round, so they need to be robust too. What is important to me is atmosphere. Having chosen to model a narrow gauge railway set in rural north Lincolnshire, I want it to look like the sleepy backwater it would have been, with its own way of doing things, its own style and rustic charm. It does not take a great deal of effort to add just enough detail to bring the railway to life. A few sacks on the platform waiting to be loaded, the village bobby standing by the station gate, a porter with a ladder about to change the mantle in a station gas lamp. You get the picture.

The station can't be seen from the house or upper patio, since it is against the lower patio wall. It is 6ft 6ins (2M) long and 3ft wide, which seemed quite large until the track and trains arrived! The shorter of the two platforms is 5ft (1.5M) long, just enough for a short passenger train. Despite being not much more than a halt, it looks quite impressive, boasting two buildings with waiting rooms, a station building with offices and a ladies waiting room and a stationmaster's house. Water cranes, station furniture and enamel advertising signs complete the scene. East of the station is a siding with a coaling stage and water tower, and beyond that a signal box. The main line heads round to the south while a spur goes straight on to a curve leading into the shed. To the west, the line heads off over the truss bridge, with a spur to another siding.

Whistle, Sharp Curve, Beware of Trains

In the southeast corner of the garden, the 6ft high stone built wall meets a tall evergreen hedge. Since not much would grow close to the hedge, this was chosen for a small industrial scene, with a halt and sidings. Originally, a wood yard was planned, but the purchase of factory buildings from Tuxcraft changed this notion. I needed some loads for flat wagons, and Karl had some spare metal parts from abandoned models. One or two

Right: **As well as a whistle, this radio-controlled model has working draincocks. Before setting off, the exhaust can be diverted to the front underside of the locomotive, allowing any condensed water to be ejected onto the track rather than out of the chimney. The resultant steam emission looks very much like the working cylinder draincocks on the real thing.**

Lower: **This girder bridge is made of mild steel, and it amplifies the sound of the train wheels rattling over the rail joins. Very satisfying! The sidings have been covered with Rowlands mix (a mix of cement, sand and peat. This sets hard, looks realistic, and the peat will allow moss to grow). They are now getting a good covering of moss, adding greatly to the realism and atmosphere.**

were left to rust beside the sidings, and the main factory building, with its tall chimney, became a small foundry. An adjacent coal stage completed the picture. The area was covered with Rowlands mix (in my case one part cement, three parts sand and one part peat) and now has a nice covering of moss.

Around the line are a few signs, 'Whistle', 'Sharp Curve', 'Beware of Trains' etc. There is a footpath crossing on the line running west of the station, made from surplus sleepers. Line side huts are dotted around, with shovels and rakes etc leaning outside. A late addition was signals. Four home signals were made from kits, and 'fixed distants' were made from wooden posts and plastic card. A lot of people don't bother with signals; indeed they were sparse on many narrow gauge railways, but very few had none, and I like the height they lend to the railway. One day I hope to get around to having more line side fencing, which is currently only around the station. A few animals (the Early Learning Centre is good for these) are placed here and there; children love these little touches of detail.

Populating the railway is a mixture of figures. Most are 16mm scale white metal, but some are G-scale plastic ones. You can't mix these in close proximity, but in areas not too close to the trains the slightly undersized G-scale does not show. You can also use these figures in coaches, since they are only glimpsed, and in any case, real people do vary quite a lot in size!

My locomotives are a mixture of live steam and battery powered 'diesels', the latter scratch or kit built. Stock is also a mixture of kits and items I've built from scratch with plywood and plastic card, beading and channel. Dry press lettering by

Decadry, bought at a stationers, identify private owner and SWR stock. The more sophisticated lettering on the coaches is done with transfers from Garden Railway Specialists. The models are not highly detailed, but at garden railway viewing distance they pass muster, I think. The difficult bits, wheels, axle boxes and bogies come from Brandbright or IP Engineering. If I can scratch build something I reckon anyone can, and I am not being modest; all it takes is a very little ability to use simple hand tools and some patience. They might not be 'Model of the Year' contenders, but each of them has given me immense satisfaction. They are unique, because no other railway is quite like the SWR.

Weston & Wrekin Havock Light Railway

Well known for his range of 'Home & Colonial' coaches and 'Busy Body' figures for 16mm and ⅞th scale garden railways, *Rob Bennett's* own line is a delightfully quirky Ministry of Defence narrow gauge line with an early sixties feel and populated with people who would feel at home on a Donald McGill seaside postcard.

Rob himself says, "Of course this world originated in my head and, in my attempt to create it in the garden, I have found that if I'm not outside actually working on it I can see it through the window. I also see it in the car, at work, the supermarket and before I go to sleep ... Why? I've made a few other garden railways and all have held me in their spell ... it's not the fear of the big wide world that makes me create this miniature environment with its quaint railway running out of sight behind the shrubbery. I think we all have this need - us garden railwaymen anyway - to create a believable little world, maybe it's a throwback to Empire building, the need for a railway to get from A to B via C and probably A again, to provide goods and chattels and a means of transport to local people. Whatever it is there seems to be a need to own this managed, sedate and elegant steam traction in our gardens and I don't think, once you've tried it, that it's likely to leave you..."

The silence is rarely broken on the Weston under Redcastle station platform, small birds twitter, crows 'caw' and that's about it. But today is different, even though it's seven o'clock in the morning (and a bit nippy!) there is a chatting and a bustling of folk as the Weston and Wrekin Havock Light Railway preservation volunteers are arriving to breathe life into the station,

for today is the start of the 'Gala Bank Holiday Weekend' and everything needs to be ready for the first train of the day.

The society has been renovating the line for the last six years and this 1964 Gala celebration represents the second year the line has been running steam. The line's original use with the MoD's Anti Tank range at Wrekin Havock has dwindled to a

Left: **A visiting *'Jack'* style Hunslet, built by Harvey Watkins, is being fired up to help out with the day's timetable.**

Right: **The *Little Weeder* bought at auction from the Balmoral Estates Railway, a line created for the old King's shootin'pals, but which closed as the presence of the bar coach reduced shooting accuracy.**

Lower: **The open Simplex makes its way through the cutting, one of the first duties of the day is to send the maintenance train off to check the line for debris, tree falls, leaves or anything one of our six cats may have inadvertently left there.**

dawdle and there is only a small military presence on the range run by the Major. The range is still in operation, but down at the camp the carpenters in the Target Shed now take on a few freelance jobs from the local villagers and outside concerns, and the once busy sand quarry line that used to take sand up to the target sites on the range, now caters for the building trade in the area...so there's a nice bit of spare cash floating around for the boys down at the range...to be spent on a few of life's little luxuries.

By nine o'clock the station is functioning and the first passengers and 'gricers' are arriving for the day. As they filter out from the ticket office onto the platform, the sun sparkles through the trees onto Nick's Tea stall situated at the end of the 'up line' platform. Mona, Nick's young waitress (her words not Nick's, he thinks she does more loitering than catering) leans inside the tea stall doorway, one arm just about folded under her ample charms, cradling the other with hand lolling and fag attached. Staring off into the distance she's wondering if that nice young corporal from the camp will be taking her to the Gala Dance tonight at the QM's stores - behind her, on the hot stove, the kettle starts to turn black.

Mona's Stocking Tops

There's a good few on the platform now and eager faces shielding their squinting eyes from the early morning sun, look down the line towards Wrekin Havock to catch a glimpse of the first train coming up the line. A whistle is heard and a cheer goes up as *Myfannwy* a small 0-4-0 Decauville comes into view steaming up the bank, making a satisfying chuff as she does so. The train

Left: Early preservation volunteers on the sawmill road with the Decauville in steam.

Lower: Another view of the Sawmill road, here you can see the work that is needed to clear the line so that log trains can get in and out to take much needed supplies of wood down to the carpenters shed at Wrekin Range. They have just started a new line in furniture down there 'Cheap and Chippendale' seems to be a real little earner down in London's Mayfair...

is made from two Quarryman's coaches and a sheep wagon converted to take passengers. This was kindly built and donated by the boys down at the range (for ulterior motives) the seating being two pews donated by the vicar of Wrekin Parva as a thanks to the line for supplying a bigger flock to his small chapel. The 'Evensong Express' was a big hit with the local villagers and brought trainloads of parishioners from down the line - although the conversion from a sheep wagon did make some giggle. But today the sun is out and it's going to be glorious.

The train is coming through the station now and you can feel, as the engine passes, the heat from the firebox and smell

the steam, oil and coal. Coaches roll past the eye and, as they gently come to a standstill, doors are flung open, the crowd on the platform pile into the coaches and, once inside, they await the guard's whistle to send them off up the line. Out of the left-hand windows passengers enjoy the view of the blue and distant hills of the Long Mynd near Church Stretton, while out of the right the passengers can enjoy the glorious view of Mona's stocking tops as she rummages under the counter for some smoky bacon crisps. Whistle blown, a little jolt and they're off - the little Decauville pulling hard as the happy faces and waving hands move out into the Shropshire countryside.

The track stretches off into the distance, the heat of the day has warmed the sleepers and they give off a heady aroma. I had decided to hand-build the track, cutting all the sleepers and steeping them in a mix of environmentally friendly creosote and old sump oil. The rail is flat bottomed, spiked to the sleepers and sits in a ballast of granite chippings. All of the prototypes on my railway are on the small side, old WW1 wagons, skips and quarrymen's coaches. The Decauville *Maude* is an 0-4-0, based on the one in the Volos brick works in Greece, *Myfannwy* is helping out whilst on its way to America and both were built by Harvey Watkins. The Dewinton *Dewi*, built by Richard Ough, operates mostly down at the Range and is only small but a good hauler, taking the skips full of sand up to the target area. There is also a scratch-built Ruston, and a Simplex built by Outline models. As I model in a scale of ⅞ins to the foot on this railway, it is quite satisfying to add all the detail, rivet and bolt detail shows up well in this scale. The railway blends well into the plantings around the line and a rake of seven skips trundling slowly through the cutting I have made in the slope of the lawn looks very effective.

Apart from Gala days and Bank Holidays, when engines arrive from other lines for a steam up and camera call - there is always something going round, maintenance trains and weeding for instance is a happy chore as the battery locos take wagon loads of weeds away in the WW1 bogie wagons and the maintenance crew trundle off up the line for a light lunch and a snooze on the embankment...sadly the will to work is weak. The Sawmill has been busy of late however and a good few trees in the wood have been felled, transported to the sawmill, and found their way, via the circular saw, down to the carpenters shed on the range.

It's a good half an hour journey back down to Wrekin Havock and, as we arrive there are waving squaddies having a fag behind the gate house as we pass, some are painting stones around the gate and others are happy to sit outside the target shed playing cards. At this point I think you should know a bit about the range and so here is an extract taken from the Wrekin 'Bugle' written by local historian Major Richard Ough (Ret).

A Short History of Wrekin Havoc Ranges

The Wrekin dominates the Shropshire plain, and if one looks at its North side whilst driving along the A5 trunk road, the observant will notice an apparent slot in the woods and undergrowth. This is the last vestige of a series of ranges built in the early 1940s to cater for the Army's needs during the Second World War.

During the early stages of the war it was obvious that German successes on the battlefield lay in their superior tank capabilities. The only anti-tank weapons that the British Army could muster were the Boys (0.5ins) anti-tank rifle and the Two Pound (40mm) anti-tank gun, which were ineffectual against the German armour plate. This state of affairs could not be allowed to continue, so the decision was taken to create a specialist trials unit where anti-tank weapons with much improved armour penetration capabilities could be developed.

A few miles to the North East of the Wrekin, the Army was already developing the huge Ordnance Depot complex at Donnington. Here they had requisitioned the narrow gauge South Horton Irrigation Tramway, and its use had considerably speeded up the construction of the Depot. This virtually unknown line had originally been built to aid the construction of a series of land drains in the 1920s, and was still using ex WW1 surplus WD locos and rolling stock.

Now any military range requires lots of space for indirect fire such as mortar or artillery. For direct fire one needs something to stop the rounds disappearing down range and landing in inconvenient places. Large quantities of rubble are required for building up the range roads and various hard standing areas while sand is needed at backstops and on small arms ranges. Fuel and water are needed for vehicles and wash down points.

Weston Redstone Quarries Limited already operated a road stone crushing plant near Wrockwardine, and they already had

WREKIN HAVOCK PRESERVES ITS LITTLE RAILWAY

At weeken[d] train . Since family estate quarry, he is society can ru[n]. At weekends a train . Since 'Cr[usty'] family estate in quarry, he is v[ery] society can ru[n]. At weekends train . Since family esta[te] quarry, he[re] society ca[n]

MORE STEAM ENGINE[S] TO RUN ON LI[NE]

At weekends a local railway preservation group run the occasional train . Since 'Crusty' owns a De Winton steam locomotive from the family estate in North Wales where it had been used in a small slate quarry, he is very amenable to their cause. As a result of this, the society can run trains up to Neves Castle.

a two-foot gauge railway to move their products to the GWR main line at Allscott, where there was a transfer yard. A little further to the East there were a few viable sandpits. With the military effort ongoing at Donnington, and the natural 'back stop' created by the Wrekin, the scene was set.

It was decided that if this scheme was to succeed then the provision of a reliable transport system was paramount. With the obvious success of requisitioning the railway at Donnington, the WD decided to do likewise with the Weston undertaking. However, it was soon apparent to the RE survey team that visited the area that the quarry railway ran in the wrong direction. Undeterred by this the team did conclude that a combined railhead at Allscott was a distinct possibility, and that by making an end on connection to the quarry concern, trains could run direct from quarry to ranges without transfer. Likewise the Army could extend the existing exchange yard at Allscott to meet their needs.

This compromise led to all round approval and construction began soon after. The Army extended the Allscott facilities, and established a loco depot and a workshop just to the south of the GWR mainline, but it soon became apparent that the distance between Allscott and the range sites was too far to facilitate effective command and control. A further decision was made to requisition a farm complex at Wrekin Havock to act as the administrative centre. With the exception of the farmhouse, which was used as the Officers Mess, the rest of the outbuildings were razed to the ground and a small, purpose built camp erected in its place.

At the end of hostilities, the ranges continued to be used for trials purposes, although for the majority of the time it was used as a trade training camp for conscripts. Here they were to discover the delights of railway operation in a different

A WW1 bogie wagon from the requisitioned South Horton Irrigation Tramway. This virtually unknown line had originally been built to aid the construction of a series of land drains in the 1920's and was still using ex WW1 surplus WD locos and rolling stock many years later.

context to the standard gauge operations at Longmoor in the south of England.

The 1960s saw the cessation of conscription and the decline of military operations. Better training bases were readily available in BAOR and at BATUS in Canada, and despite protests from the MoD, the new Labour Defence minister ordered the closure of a large number of smaller military units, which included the experimental ranges at the base of the Wrekin.

I thank Richard for this insight into Wrekin Havock as I would never have been able to reconstruct this wonderful line in my garden and in exhibition layout form without him. There are still a few old timers who remember the days at the Range who sit in the Public Bar of the 'Bullet Hole' at Wrekin Parva and I thank them too for all their fond memories - they have given me, so many stories you could write a book.

The Spirit of Compton Down

Peter Jones was a war baby born in the blitzed ruins of Portsmouth. Cheerfully obsessed with railways from the moment he drew his first breath, his seminal visit to the Talyllyn Railway in 1948 is well documented and eventually resulted in the first CDR started in 1949. Brought up close to Fratton shed (70F) Peter eventually studied music but let down the side by becoming a rock musician in the 1960s. He also rescued old railway engines, buildings and structures as a hobby. Eventually moving to the tranquillity of West Wales, Peter stayed with music and garden railways (see thejudyjonesband.com). In 1975 he moved to a house with a secure back garden and started planning the final form of the CDR. In 1999, fifty years of the Compton Down Railway (in various formats) was celebrated.

My own memories of the CDR are encapsulated in the poetic and evocative writings of Peter Jones which, when I first read of the doings at Compton Down in *16mm Today*, made an immediate impact. You see not only was this railway presented as if it was a real Victorian enterprise...complete right down to timetables and local newspaper, but his methods of design and construction Peter made very accessible to tyro's such as myself. My own Longlands & Western Railway, while absolutely nothing like the enterprise at Compton Down, is based on many of the principles forged by Peter Jones during the construction of this famous railway. For instance both lines live in the real world of wind and weather - structures, signals and buildings do not come in for the winter and are not 'posed' in position for a running session. The different qualities of light and weather make a garden railway (rather than a model railway in the garden) attractive to look at even during the dankest of winter days...

The Compton Down Railway, ah yes... things are a little different here. There is an elusive difference between a garden railway and a model railway in a garden. The boundary between the two is hazy but the CDR is firmly in the second group. As much as possible, everything in the garden is suborned to the cause of railway atmosphere and realism. But it still all happens under the ever-changing play of light and season. It is a different railway every day. In a sense, it isn't even a model railway: the track that wanders through the landscape just happens to be of a very small gauge.

But this is the dreamer in me talking. We really ought to concentrate on more tangible things. So first; a brief history. The very first CDR started in 1949 - inspired by a trip to the Talyllyn Railway by a very small boy. The result was tinplate track set permanently into rockeries, together with clockwork engines and rolling stock clothed in larger narrow gauge bodies. By pure accident, I had entered the world of 16mm scale narrow gauge. Track was ballasted with ashes or soil, and simple trains were run. The joy of just seeing rail-tops winding through slightly overgrown surroundings was born... and has remained ever since.

The workmanship was not of the best but the trains ran. Variations of this system gave pleasure for some years. Better rolling stock was built and it was a rewarding, if somewhat solitary, pursuit. Then, of course, came the inevitable inter-

Gazing down on a drab waterworks siding, we see the humdrum, everyday part of railways: not much glamour here.

Above: **Minster Road is the main station on a light tramway that has a rural, bucolic feel to it. The management of the CDR tend to leave this little railway to its own devices.**

Left: **The Kerr Stuart tank engine is silent on a Sunday morning. Tomorrow the work will begin all over again, but for now, peace reigns.**

vention of teenage and the attractions it had to offer. But the CDR soldiered on in the background. However, in time the pull was too great to resist and track was laid. The journey was renewed gently until... in 1979 there was the opportunity to really get stuck in to a wilderness of a garden that had the benefit of being secure. If I was going to build a garden railway, said I to myself, why not take the opportunity to try out all

sorts of ideas that had been floating about in the dimmer recesses of my mind for ages, and make it a good 'un.

Perception of Narrowgaugeness

The site is 70ft x 40ft and vaguely flat. The track layout is nearly a complete circuit but not quite: two termini are adjacent to

each other. I don't like ground level operation but I do like ground level realism. So most of the system is built on big raised areas - about waist height - fronted by stone or brick walls. This was a major undertaking but proved wise with the passing years. The termini are set on substantial timber bases. The majority of the railway remains faithful to my beloved 16mm scale on 32mm gauge track (SM32). But there is also some 45mm gauge track as well. This system is also in 16mm scale and so is different to the concept of G-scale. In order to 'make the narrow gauge look narrow gauge' there is a modest amount of 2½ins gauge 'standard gauge' track and stock. This really improves the perception of the narrowgaugeness of the CDR. This is difficult to convey in words but is obvious when you see it.

Trackwork is a total mixture of bits and pieces going back many years. Much of it is Peco but there is also quite a bit of Tenmille. To cure the tendency of pop-in chairs to pop out, there are some small pins applied at about every fourth sleeper. Careful looking will reveal some traditional type track here and there. The 45mm gauge track is mostly Peco gauge-1 track with alternate sleepers removed. This gives the matching delicate look of 16mm narrow gauge. There is some cruder G-scale track in use (because I had some), but I would like to phase that out with time. There are also some sections of the railway that are modelled on very light industrial systems and here Peco 7mm scale track is used. It is mostly deeply inset into concrete and so the under-scale sleepers are not noticeable.

The basic track layout is very simple indeed - just a simple end-to-end thing between the two big stations. But the complexity comes because of the ancillary systems everywhere. Where the big quarry is located, there are four levels to juggle with. I like to use height to add to the drama and impact of a layout. The highest gallery is approximately six foot high, whereas the lowest track is down at ankle height. The complete railway lets me operate the line in different ways. On a few occasions it has been run to timetable operation, observing rules and regulations. But this has mostly been for the pleasure of others and not mine.

Splendidly Irrational

It also functions as a partly successful track for visitors to run their trains on. However, it has to be said that it is not geared up for big social events. Its main *raison d'etre* is in being something very personal to me. Here is a world of narrow gauge atmosphere where trains run as and when I want them to. Usually they are live steam hauled, but there is plenty of battery power in evidence. You will look in vain for evidence of two-rail operation or radio control. I ask my trains to be free spirits. However, in some small industrial workings there may be some automatic shuttling to and fro going on, leaving me to concentrate on running the main trains. The garden is arranged so that it is impossible to see the entire railway from any one place. Indeed, mostly it consists of glimpses of cameos. I should explain that the garden has a high railway content anyway. It is my open-air 'railway room' and there is a lot of furniture in it.

"To me, garden railways are an art, not a science"

Above: **An Archangel** *'Brick'*
dwarfs the small bogie van it is
shunting at Llanbedr Road.

My collection of locomotives is splendidly irrational. There are far too many engines, but I've built or bought them over many years and they have remained with me. The oldest working engine on the line is the battery powered *'Welsh Pony'*. This was originally built in 1953, the body being mostly built of card. It has had many repairs and mods done down the decades, but still has a run from time to time. The motor in it dates from the 1930s and I try and restrict its 'life hours' these days. There is a replica of the very first CDR loco - built for my 50th anniversary in 1999 - around a Hornby clockwork tank engine. I have tried to compile lists of engines past and present, but the time taken is better spent running trains! There are usually

Above: **The slag siding of the ironworks is not the most picturesque of locations.**

Right: **Up in the slate quarry, a couple of wagons show the natural weathering caused by standing out in the open for twenty years.**

between 6-10 live steam engines around the place and somewhere around 50 battery locos. You see what I mean about 'irrational'!

Rolling stock is equally eclectic and the stock list just sort of 'grewed' over the years. There are lots of tiny vehicles, in deplorable condition, to be found in the quarries and industries. There are also the biggies up on the main line. There have long been plans for building proper rakes of this

or that but not much has happened yet. This is certainly the weakest area of the CDR.

Realism of the Ordinary

So far, these words have dealt with the nuts and bolts common to many garden railways. But what defines the CDR is its search for

Above: Shafts of early morning summer sunlight stream into Compton Brickworks. Steam is just being raised. You can smell the hot steam oil and hear the sounds of steam engines coming to life.

Left: The old sawmill at Minster Road sees a rail delivery. It brightens up this dull November afternoon.

Right: The mid-morning down train bursts out of Castle Tunnel. The locomotive is a 're-imported North British Loco 2-6-4 that had been built for export'.

Lower: Parts of the old Brickworks are giving cause for concern. Decades of excavation have rendered the ground unstable in places.

'the realism of the ordinary'. There are plenty of industries and there is much that is unspectacular but on a grand scale. Colours are muted and there is a lot of emphasis on a railway in all weathers. A dull morning in February is as important as the brighter sunny days. There is some external lighting and the railway is available for use 24/7/365. Many of the buildings are based on old industrial structures (mostly long since disappeared) I sketched as a youth. There is a brickworks, an ironworks and a waterworks tucked away. There is large quarrying activity and an enclosed dock basin with shipbuilding activity. At the time of writing, a coking plant and steelworks is under construction. I enjoy the challenge of making buildings that work. So I can make 16mm scale bricks in the brickworks, for example. The waterworks pumps and purifies water, splendidly gurgling and splashing as it does so.

So there are plenty of opportunities for steam and smoke to drift over the landscape to let the light play in ever changing ways. And this is at the very heart of what I want from the CDR. The garden is that other world: the place where they do things differently. It is the place where things happen as and when I want them to. I enjoy the artistic, creative process. It would be a bad day if ever the railway were finished. But fortunately, this is an impossibility. Over the years I have made many mistakes. I have tried to raise my standards. Most of all, newer ideas have come to me. It is not logical but is possessed of infinite satisfaction. I'll settle for that...